# Autopsy of a Dead Church

# CSI: Church Status Investigation

***Creative and Challenging Insights That Will Help You and Your Church Stay Out of the Spiritual Obituaries***

**by**

**Lou Mancari**

Illustrations by Stephanie Todoroff

Xulon Press

*Autopsy of a Dead Church*
by Lou Mancari

Printed in the United States of America

ISBN 1-60034-025-3



www.xulonpress.com

# Dedication

To my
**Lord and Savior**
**Jesus Christ**
**The Head of the Church**

and

To my loving wife, the godly mother of our children,
and my best friend
**Iris**
Your beauty is from the inside out.
No man could have a more faithful companion.
Thank you for believing this book was possible.

# Acknowledgments

I want to say thanks to my precious children: Amber Joy, Rebecca Grace, Christal Hope, and Luke Daniel. You have cheered me on in this project and in all of life. There is no sweeter word to my ears than "Daddy," as spoken from your lips. What a privilege and honor to have that position in your life.

Thanks to my father and mother who have unconditionally loved me. You have given me roots from which to draw strength. And thanks for being wonderful grandparents to my children.

Thank you to Christal Hoo for all the editing work you have done on the raw copy of this manuscript. You and your mother have been our loyal friends for over twenty years. And Stephanie Todoroff, your sketches are great, and I am honored that you were willing to invest your talent in this book.

I appreciate my fellow mission workers at Gospelink, especially our director, Lewis Nelms, for teaching me about foreign missions. I miss your daily fellowship, our prayer meetings, and your "beautiful feet."

Thanks to each of the individuals and churches that have supported my family as missionaries with Gospelink. You have made it possible for me to do the ministry I love and truly believe in.

The original idea for this book first came to me in 1981. I heard Dr. Jack Hyles, who was at the time my pastor, mention that as a young preacher he once preached a message titled "The Autopsy of a Dead Church". I have never read or heard that sermon but I always thought it would be a great theme to develop. If anything in this book seems to correspond to his original message it is completely unintentional.

Some of Dr. James M. Boice's lectures were used as substantial source material for chapter 5 and John H. Armstrong's lectures on the Theology of the Cross were vital sources used for chapter 9.

Finally, I would like to thank Pastor John Briggs and all our friends at Blessed Hope Bible Church of Liverpool, Pennsylvania. Your friendship and generous support over the years has made it possible for many national preachers to be helped. Also, for almost fifteen years we learned together about the local church of Jesus Christ. I will forever be honored to know that I was once your pastor.

# Table of Contents

# Preface

# Why This Book, at This Time?

> And unto the Angel of the church in Sardis write: These things saith He that hath the seven stars; I know thy works, that thou hast a name that thou livest, and art dead.—Rev. 3:1

On March 30, 2005, I celebrated my fiftieth birthday. It was also my twenty-fifth year as a Christian. I have been a preacher of the glorious gospel of Jesus Christ for twenty-three years. For almost eighteen of those years, I have been a Bible-preaching church planter and pastor. I love the local church and the Lord of the church, who gave His life for the church. This is the primary reason for writing this book.

I have walked the gang-infested streets of South Chicago, preaching and teaching the Bible. For several of those years my young bride, Iris, would stand by my side as I shared the Word of God with Mexican immigrants, and she would translate the message into Spanish. I would walk by dead, empty churches along the streets. My heart would grieve over the large church buildings that once held such hope for spiritually sick and dead souls, but now these churches are as dead as any corpse in the city morgue. Granted, they may distribute some food and beverages to the needy, for which I thank God, but they no longer dispense the Bread of Life or the

Living Water. Sad to say, they only help the streets of Chicago be a little better place from which the lost will go to hell.

I have walked the streets of New York City sharing the gospel. I have knocked on the doors of over twenty thousand homes on Staten Island and in Brooklyn. I have been cursed at, spit on, ignored, chased by dogs (I have observed that pit bulls and Dobermans are the preference of the drug dealers), threatened with a baseball bat, had a switchblade pointed at my nose, and even had a gun placed in my face.

Yet, one of the saddest things about New York City to me is when I recall some of the large, ornate stone church buildings that are to this day dead with religion. I experienced this firsthand when we were attempting to find a building where we could bring people we had won to Christ from the projects of north Staten Island. Because we were a new independent Bible church, we did not yet have our own building. Church after church would refuse to allow us to use their empty buildings because we were not wearing their religious labels. We did finally find a Unitarian church that allowed us to rent their building on Sunday evenings. (They barely used it on Sunday mornings themselves.) What an exciting experience to see that old building come alive every Sunday night with the laughter and singing of redeemed white, Hispanic, black, and Asian adults and children.

After we left New York City, my family and I moved to rural central Pennsylvania. Perry County, Pennsylvania, does not have a traffic light in the whole county. I often have said, "Perry County has more deer than people, but the people are dear." There we began with a few people around our kitchen table and started the Blessed Hope Bible Church. We saw the church grow from my kitchen to our whole house within the first year. We then rented a couple of rooms at a local grange hall. After our second year, we needed to rent the whole grange. Within a few more years we purchased a piece of property and built a new church building. For three years, we met only in the basement of that building so as to save on construction costs. In 1998, we finished the full construction of that church building.

During those years of steady church growth, I spent countless hours in study of God's Word for my personal growth; oftentimes I would dedicate twenty hours a week or more to sermon preparation. I have preached expositional sermons through fifty-four books of the Bible. There were several years when I would read a book or two and sometimes three a week. I have listened to well over a thousand sermons on tape by men of many different backgrounds and theological persuasions. This does not include what I have heard on the radio or at a conference.

As a sidebar, I have been rebuked by a couple of self-proclaimed prophets for reading commentaries. Their eyes roll and tongues cluck whenever they see more than a dozen books in one room. These same folks preach sermon after sermon and sell their tapes to anyone who will buy them. All of these sermons are, in effect, a commentary on the text from which they are preaching. Unless the preacher gets up in the pulpit and reads the Bible text only, what you end up with is a commentary, whether written or oral. I make no apology for studying what other Christians have learned. The Holy Spirit certainly has been actively teaching others for over two thousand years. Why not glean from what He has taught others? Proverbs 24:11 tells us, "Where no counsel is, the people fall: but in the multitude of counselors there is safety."

I have read the Calvinist and the Arminian. I have read the Puritans and the contemporary church-growth gurus. I have read the fundamentalist Baptist and the Charismatic. I have read copious volumes produced by the Presbyterians and even some from the Pentecostals. I have read from Finney to Falwell, from Hyles to Hybels. I have read from Bob Jones to Martyn-Loyd Jones, from Warren Wiersbe to Rick Warren. I have read and listened to John MacArthur and John Maxwell. I have studied sermons from Sproul to Stanley, from Chuck Swindoll to Charles Spurgeon. I have gleaned from Augustine to Zacharias and literally, from Peter, Paul, Piper, and Pink. I have been to both Jack Hyles' Pastor's School and James M. Boice's Reform Conference. I have been to Bill Gothard's conferences and Bill Gaither's concerts.

Since I have worked in missions with Gospelink, I have preached in about twenty types of denominational churches (if you count the different types of Baptist churches). During my Christian life, I have been in well over one hundred churches across America, eight other countries, and four continents.

During these years, I have been consciously and subconsciously absorbing the material about the church and the Christian life that I am now setting forth on these pages. I will share first and foremost what I believe the Bible says about the character of the church and her people. Secondly, I will share what other people of God have said and written over the years. If I remember where I have learned something I will seek to give that person credit. If I am not sure where I have heard it then I ask that person's indulgence. Anything in this book original with me may be used and quoted to further God's Kingdom without any credit or mention of this author. Thirdly, I will share from what I have learned from speaking with some of my contemporary pastors and evangelists. And lastly, I will share what the Lord has taught me personally through my walk and work with Him.

I am fully aware that some of the things I write will make some people I know very unhappy or at least uncomfortable with me. This brings me no joy, and I pray that they will not choose to break fellowship with me over some issue that I regard as a non-essential. I do not pretend to have all the answers or to be always right. I have lived long enough to know that there are so many things I do not know. Also, over the years there are things that I have changed my mind about as the Lord's Word has edified my conscience. I reserve the right to allow God the Holy Spirit to change my mind about any subject as He illuminates my understanding of His Holy Bible. Our Lord is so very gracious, kind, and patient with us! I trust we can all learn from Him.

I have struggled to start this book, because I want everything that I say to be right. Perfection is a worthy goal but not very practical. I have finally come to the conclusion that if I wait until I am right about everything I will never write about anything!

May I repeat myself? I am writing this book first of all because I love the local church and her Lord. The church is where I have learned of salvation through my Lord and Savior Jesus Christ. It is in the church where I first sang the hymns and choruses that often bring truth to my mind and joy to my heart. The church is where I was baptized. The church is where I was called to preach and where I met and married my wife. The church is where I was licensed to preach and ordained as a pastor. The church was my children's home away from home. The church is where friends, deacons, and Sunday school teachers became extended family members. The church is where I baptized all four of our children and buried our first son, Jeremiah. The church is where I have served for these past twenty years of full-time ministry. The church people have been the avenue by which God has supplied my family's earthly needs. The local churches in America are the life blood of our mission work at Gospelink. I love the church.

However, many churches in America are in deep trouble. They are like the church mentioned by our Lord in Revelation 3:1, quoted at the beginning of this chapter. Revelation 3:1-6 tells us the church at Sardis had a reputation before men as being great and even doing some good works but in God's eyes had become dead. The church was populated with unregenerate spiritual zombies. They were animated with deeds but dead of spiritual substance. The Lord does leave them with hope. He commends a few people there who have been faithful. He then tells the rest of the church to wake up and hold on to the doctrines that they still have but have placed on the back burner. Then He tells them to repent and remember the truth that they have ignored or disregarded altogether. There is hope for the dead church to be revived.

The words that follow on these pages are meant to help us and to cultivate hope. Some of these issues I have failed at and am still seeking the victory over. As pastor of a church for many years, I certainly did not always meet the standards that I have set forth here. However, if we are honest and open-hearted to the Lord, we have to admit that we learn more from our failures than from our triumphs. I would have to agree with one of my favorite comic characters, Charlie Brown, in his response to such a statement: "That must make me one of the smartest people in the world."

Most of what I write will not be new truth to many people, but perhaps if told in a somewhat different way, that old truth may find new meaning and personal application. Jesus said, "You shall know the truth and the truth shall set you free." It is the application of the truth that is our source of true freedom, not just the knowledge of truth. Notice Jesus did not say, "You shall know the truth and be free."

Secondly, I am writing this book now because I am at a point in my life when people often take inventory of where they have been.

While doing that, I cannot get this burden off my chest that has been there for several years. Whether anyone will listen is yet to be known, but I must speak what I have seen and heard.

Thirdly, the analogy of the autopsy is obviously everywhere in the media today. Several of the most-viewed TV shows in the past few years have been based on this theme. I pray that the "CSI" on the cover will draw some readers who might not ordinarily read a book in this genre. Hence, the timing of this book is culturally and socially relevant.

Finally, 20-50 percent of all the profits made on this book will go directly into foreign missions through Gospelink or any local church purchasing more than fifty books.

# I Love Thy Kingdom, Lord

I love Thy kingdom, Lord
The house of Thine abode,
The Church our blest Redeemer saved,
With His own Blood.

I love Thy Church, O God!
Her walls before Thee stand,
Dear as the apple of Thine eye,
And graven on Thy hand.

For her my tears shall fall;
For her my prayers ascend;
To her my cares and toils be giv'n,
Till toils and cares shall end.

—Timothy Dwight

# Christ Pictures His Church

Even as Christ is the head of the church: and he is the Savior of the body.—Eph. 5:23

For as we have many members in one body, and all members have not the same office: so we, being many, are one body in Christ, and every one members one of another.—Rom. 12:4-5

# Introduction

# Christ Pictures His Church

A prominent Bible teacher once made this statement, "It should be against the law to bore people with the Bible." I could not agree more! I have been in the company of some preachers who seem to think it a sin to illustrate a passage of Scripture either from their personal life, history, or a parable. They somehow equate bland, colorless intellectualism with spirituality. Perhaps it is a latent need to do and dispense penance. Their preaching and teaching reminds me of the old black-and-white Dragnet detective series in which Sgt. Joe Friday, played by Jack Webb, would say to the witness in a monotone voice, "Just the facts, sir." The Bible is factual and true, but it is more than a bunch of facts that are true. It is alive and life-giving!

The Bible is the greatest book the world has ever known or will ever know. It is not boring, and neither should we be boring in teaching it. Jesus was certainly not afraid to take real-life illustrations from what He observed around Him. He used corn, wheat, water, bread, soil, light, and more to bring home His truth to His disciples. If we want to be a dynamic, vital teacher of God's Word, we need to use illustrations as well. While speaking about the church (the church as represented by all Christians as well as the local churches), the Lord used several pictures to make His particular points. The church is referred to as a sheepfold with the Lord Jesus as the Shepherd (John 10:7-16). The church is described as a building with many stones, including the chief cornerstone, Jesus Christ (1 Pet. 2:4-8). The church is pictured as the bride of Christ

(Eph. 5:22-33). The church is likened to a family or household with many different members and God as the Father (Matt. 6:8-14; Eph. 2:19). The church is pictured as a sturdy pillar upon solid ground upholding the truth of God's Word (1 Tim. 3:14-15). Each of these portraits conjures up in our minds certain aspects of how the church functions.

This leads me to the picture of the church that I will seek to develop in the following chapters of this book.

**The Church as a Body**

> For as the body is one, and hath many members, and all the members of that one body, being many, are one body: so also is Christ. And whether one member suffer, all the members suffer with it; or one member be honoured, all the members rejoice with it. Now ye are the body of Christ, and members in particular.—1 Cor. 12:12, 26-27

> And he gave some, apostles; and some, prophets; and some, evangelists; and some, pastors and teachers; for the perfecting of the saints, for the work of the ministry, for the edifying of the body of Christ.—Eph. 4:11-12

These scriptures clearly depict the church of Jesus Christ as a body, with each person representing different members or parts of the body. Each part of the body has a unique and important function that helps the rest of the body. Each member is united to the other parts, and if one suffers, the whole body suffers. Notice there is unity without uniformity. The parts are united in their corporate functions, but that does not mean they are uniform in their function. They look and act differently as individual parts but work in concert with each other to make the body perform correctly. So too, we as parts of the body of Christ have different gifts and abilities (not uniformed) but work together (in unity) for the glory of God and the good of His church.

There is a less familiar text of the Old Testament that God uses to depict His people, the nation of Israel. We see in this text the people of God pictured as a sick, unhealthy body that is stricken with disease from head to toe. This sickness is, of course, essentially the spiritual decay and decadence of the people. My charismatic brethren need to keep Isaiah 1:4-6 in mind while drawing dogmatic conclusions about Isaiah 53:5. Put into the context of the book of Isaiah, the sickness, and subsequent need for healing, referred to the spiritual condition of God's people and is not a claim for physical healing. I do believe God heals people, but this is not my proof text.

> A sinful nation, a people laden with iniquity, a seed of evildoers, children that are corrupters: they have forsaken the LORD, they have provoked the Holy One of Israel unto anger, they are gone away backward. Why should ye be stricken any more? ye will revolt more and more: the whole head is sick, and the whole heart faint. From the sole of the foot even unto the head there is no soundness (health) in it; but wounds, and bruises, and putrefying sores: they have not been closed, neither bound up, neither mollified (soothed) with ointment.—Isa. 1:4-6

Now that we have established a biblical pattern for viewing the church as a body we are almost ready to perform an autopsy on a church that has died an untimely death. Before we do that, however, in the next chapter I would like us to consider some helps to maintain an individual's healthy spiritual body. The church is made up of individual Christians; hence we need to know what keeps them healthy. If one individual member is unable or unwilling to fulfill their part for the body's function, then the whole body suffers.

Dizzy Dean was one of the greatest baseball pitchers of all time. In 1937, while he was pitching in an All-Star game, he was hit by a scorching line drive that broke his toe. Strangely enough, that broken toe eventually ruined Dizzy's throwing arm. Dizzy altered his throwing motion so as to compensate for the broken toe. He was never quite the pitcher he was before. Isn't it interesting to observe how one seemingly unrelated, little member of Dizzy Dean's body affected another part of his body and eventually had an effect on his whole person?

That is how the body of Christ works. If one person does not do his part, no matter how small it might seem, it puts extra strain on another part of the body of Christ. Some people try to overcompensate and tend to become frustrated. All manner of trouble can develop. Let us all do our part by keeping spiritually healthy.

## In Christ There Is No East or West

In Christ there is no East or West,
In Him no South or North,
But one great fellowship of love,
Thru-out the whole wide earth.

In Him shall true hearts everywhere,
Their high communion find;
His service is the golden cord,
Close binding all mankind.

Join hands then, brothers of the faith,
What-e'er your race may be;
Who serves my Father as a son,
Is surely kin to me.

In Christ now meet both East and West,
In Him meet South and North;
All Christly souls are one in Him,
Thru-out the whole wide earth.

—John Oxenham

# The Anatomy of a Healthy Body

For ye are bought with a price: therefore glorify God in your body, and in your spirit, which are God's.—1 Cor. 6:20

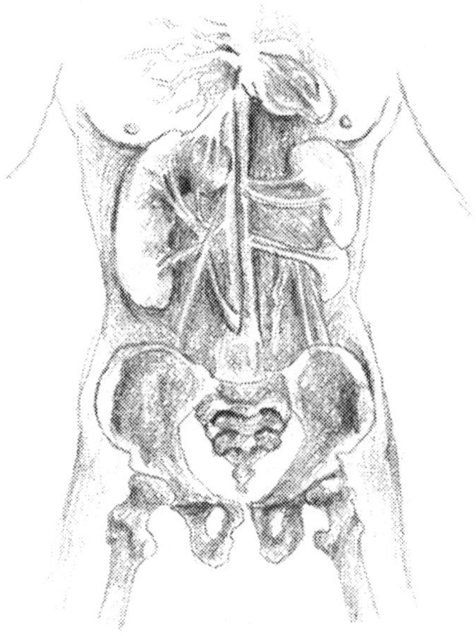

The human body is probably the most amazing example of teamwork anywhere. Every part needs the other. When the stomach is hungry, the eyes spot the hamburger. The nose smells the onions, the feet run to the snack stand, the hands douse the burger with mustard and shove it back into the mouth, where it goes down to the stomach. Now that's cooperation!—Joni Eareckson Tada

## Chapter 1

# The Anatomy of a Healthy Body

Yes, indeed, the human body is an amazing specimen of detailed cooperation. For it to function at its ultimate potential, we need to bring our physical bodies into the subjection of the Holy Spirit. The apostle Paul reminds us of this in 1 Corinthians 9:27, which states, "But I keep under my body, and bring it into subjection: lest that by any means, when I have preached to others, I myself should be a castaway." Oswald Chambers expresses this same truth: "We have to treat the body as the servant of Jesus Christ: when the body says, 'Sit,' and He says, 'Go,' go! When the body says, 'Eat,' and He says, 'Fast,' fast! When the body says, 'Yawn, and He says, 'Pray,' pray!" We can all agree that Spirit control and discipline are critical in maintaining our physical bodies so they may bring glory to God. But let us use some biblical terminology to see how the individual Christian can maintain his spiritual body so as to keep it functioning and coordinating with the larger body of Christ. This will produce a healthier local church and ultimately advance the kingdom of God.

We will, for the sake of illustration, equate each spiritual need with a physical requirement for good health. If you are a medical professional reading this book, please allow me some latitude and poetic license.

**Good Food (the Word and the Will of God)**

You know the old adages: "Junk in, junk out" and "You are what you eat." My dear wife, Iris, worked part-time for eight years in a health food store and diligently oversaw all that we as a family ate. Sorry to say, I did not always relish her choice of entrees; lentil loaf and whole wheat pasta curls were not high on my list of favorites. However, she was preparing consistent, healthful meals that would help her family grow strong and resist disease.

In the realm of our spiritual life, we need to have good spiritual food. This begins with the Bread of Life and the Living Water, Jesus Christ. He alone brings this new life in the heart of the believer. Without this regeneration of the heart a person will not have a spiritual appetite. I could stand in front of a corpse and eat the most tantalizing food, but that corpse would never respond in hungry desire. Its senses are dead to such stimulation. So it is with each person. Only those who have come into a saving relationship with the Incarnate Word, Jesus Christ (John 1:14), will have an appetite for the inspired Word, the Bible (1 Cor. 2:13-16). Spiritual nourishment is sustained through our interaction with the Bible.

The Bible is likened to:
Milk: 1 Cor. 3:2, Heb. 5:12, 1 Pet. 2:2
Bread: Matt. 4:4
Meat: 1 Cor. 3:2 , Heb. 5:12
Honey: Ps. 119:103

Jeremiah said that when he found God's Word, it was as food, and he ate God's words, and they brought joy and rejoicing to his heart (Jer. 15:16). Job said that God's Word was more important to him than his essential food (Job 23:12). Jesus also said, "My food is to do the will of Him who sent Me, and to finish His work" (John 4:34). Knowing God's Word and obeying God's Word makes the most nourishing meals.

I recall sitting at the dinner table as a child with lima beans in front of me. I was not allowed to leave the table until I had finished eating them. (I have always hated lima beans.) I chewed those beans on one side of my mouth and shifted them over to the other side of my mouth. I did that for what seemed like an eternity, but I would start to gag every time I started to swallow. When my mother was not looking, I spit the beans into my napkin and from there into my pocket. I was soon out the back door, and I quickly hid the evidence. Needless to say those beans did me very little good. So it is with the truth of God's Word. We cannot just taste it or sample it. We must digest it into our lives to gain the real value that it offers us.

**Trust and Obey**

When we walk with the Lord in the light of His Word,
What a glory He sheds on our way!
While we do His good will, He abides with us still
And with all who will trust and obey.
Trust and obey, for there's no other way,
To be happy in Jesus, but to trust and obey.

—John H. Sammis

**Good Air (Prayer)**

We all know the importance of getting out in the fresh air, breathing in deeply, and exhaling vigorously. Since birth, my son Luke has had problems with asthma. My wife and I have spent countless hours at his bedside as he labored just to suck in enough air to stay alive. It was always such a relief for Luke and us when his medicine would begin to take effect, enabling him to freely inhale. Air, something that so many of us take for granted, is so precious to our life. In this same way prayer is vital to the life of the believer.

*Exhale: Petition and Praise*—The believer is to pray without ceasing and never give up praying (1 Thess. 5:17; Luke 18:1). This prayer is to petition God for all our needs and to praise Him for all that He is and has done (Phil. 4:6). Prayer protects us from the temptation from within, our flesh (Mark 4:38). It protects us from the temptation from without, the evil one (Matt. 6:13; Eph. 6:10-18).

*Inhale: Meditation*—As we spend time with the Lord in prayer, He ministers to us and transforms us into His image (Acts 4:13; Rom. 8:26-29). I am convinced that there is a special wisdom, power, and joy inhaled from simply spending quiet time before the Lord (James 1:5; Ps. 16:11). Sometimes we need to be quiet before Him. The story is told about Mohandas Gandhi, the popular religious leader of India. Gandhi was approached by a pretentious young follower who glibly asked his mentor how he might know God. Gandhi was a keen observer of people and felt that the young man needed a lesson in sincerity. Gandhi led the young man over to a watering trough. He asked the man to kneel down beside the water. Gandhi proceeded to grab him by the back of the neck, pushed his head under the water, and held him there for some time. As air bubbles started to surface, Gandhi pulled the man's head back out of the water. The man gasped desperately for air. After a few seconds, Gandhi shoved the man's head back down into the water. Once again he pulled him back up. The man was gulping and frantically sucking in air. Gandhi then looked him straight in the eye and asked, "Do you want to know God? When you want to know God like you want to breathe, you will know God!"

Now I am not recommending Gandhi's theology or his teaching methods, but his sentiments are sound and actually scriptural. God told His people through the prophet Jeremiah, "Ye shall seek Me and find Me when ye shall search for Me with your whole heart" (Jer. 29:13). And the psalmist says that as the thirsty deer pants for water so does his soul long for God (Ps. 42:1). Seek God earnestly during your quiet time.

**Good Water (Holy Spirit)**

Whenever we travel to South America and Africa, we are always careful to have plenty of clean bottled drinking water. It is essential for the healthy functioning of our bodies. With the flooding of New Orleans due to Hurricane Katrina, we had a grim reminder of how desperate people can become without clean water to drink. The Bible tells us that the Holy Spirit is the washing and regenerating agent in the life of the believer (John 3:5-6; Titus 3:5-6). The Christian is cleansed and purified in the eyes of God at the moment of his salvation by the Holy Spirit. The Christian needs regular washings of the Spirit to cleanse and anoint him after times of confession and repentance (1 John 1:9). It is imperative that we not grieve or quench the Spirit (Eph. 4:30; 1 Thess. 5:19) but be filled (controlled) by the Spirit (Eph. 5:18).

**Good Elimination (Confession, Repentance, and Cleansing)**

Any good health specialist will tell you that regular elimination is vitally important for good body health. The body must be able to dispose of anything that is toxic. If there is any major malfunction in this process, the individual can have all types of other serious complications. So it is with sin that is left to build up in the life of a child of God. Sin that is not regularly confessed and repented of will build up and infect the rest of the Christian's life. There will be footholds given to the devil that can quickly develop into strongholds. We need a daily time of confession. Keep short accounts with God. It is interesting that clean water is an important ingredient in maintaining good elimination, and the Holy Spirit is the power to bring the cleansing of revival (Eph. 4:25-32). Please take note that the Lord Jesus sanctifies and purifies His church by the washing power of the Word of God (Eph. 5:25-27).

When I travel to Africa on mission trips, I am very cautious to maintain good external and internal hygiene. I try to discreetly wash my face and hands regularly throughout the day. I am careful never to drink anything that has not been factory sealed. And I am ever mindful to reapply the repellant that keeps malaria-infected mosquitoes at bay. Thank God, I have never been ill while on any of my trips overseas. I confess that I have not always been as diligent with my spiritual life. As a Christian, I need to take spiritual precautions and stay regularly cleansed before the Lord each day. The fact that the Lord has taught us to pray "Give us this day our daily bread and forgive us our sins" implies at least a daily need of taking out the spiritual garbage (Luke 11:4).

**Take Time to Be Holy**

Take time to be holy,
Speak oft with thy Lord;
Abide in Him always,
And feed on His Word.
Make friends of God's children;
Help those who are weak;
Forgetting in nothing
His blessings to seek.

Take time to be holy,
The world rushes on;
Spend much time in secret
With Jesus alone;
By looking to Jesus,
Like Him thou shalt be;
Thy friends in thy conduct
His likeness shall see.

Take time to be holy,
Let Him be thy guide,
And run not before Him,
Whatever betide;
In joy or in sorrow,
Still follow thy Lord,
And, looking to Jesus,
Still trust in His Word.

Take time to be holy,
Be calm in thy soul;
Each thought and each motive
Beneath His control;
Thus led by His Spirit
To fountains of love,
Thou soon shalt be fitted
For service above

—William D. Longstaff

**Good Exercise (Worshiping, Working, and Witnessing)**

Since the time we were children in school we have been told how important exercise is to good health. It is no secret, however, that no one ever became a great athlete by just reading a book or sitting in front of a coach who is drawing diagrams on a board. The way to become proficient at anything is to practice what we have been taught.

When I was a little boy, I watched the Wide World of Sports. The show featured all kinds of sports, and as soon as I would see something, I would dash outside with my friends and give it a try. I once watched these skaters speed across an ice pond and try to leap over as many barrels as possible. It looked like great fun to me. I promptly gathered my parents' garbage cans and lined them up with a couple of the neighbors' as well. I sprinted as fast as my legs would take me across the backyard and went airborne. I quickly landed squarely on top of the third garbage can. And I do mean "can." Back then, Rubbermaid was not yet making its plastic version. My eighty-pound bag of bones crushed that metal can. Of course, it did not belong to us, and my neighbor was less than impressed that my leaping prowess had allowed me to clear my parents' trash cans so gracefully only to make a crash landing on his. But man, that was fun—not just watching someone else doing it or talking about it, but getting out there and doing it myself!

As Christians we must be doers of the Word, not just hearers (James 1:22). Would to God we come out of our churches after hearing the Word and diligently get busy putting it into practice. We all need regular time of personal worship. This is a time of prayer and praise. This is a time when we thank God for what He has done and petition God for what we need Him to do in our lives. This is a time to read our Bible with delight, meditation, and an attitude of application for the day. It is a time to seek a principle to obey and a promise to own.

Get a good hymnal that has a variety of contemporary choruses and many of the old hymns that are rich in doctrine. Just this morning after breakfast my wife and I read and sang that great hymn "Day by Day." What a way to start the day! We all need public worship. This will be covered later, but we should have regular corporate worship with our local church. I am often encouraged spiritually at my home church in Virginia, especially when we observe the Lord's Supper. We remember our Savior's sacrifice. The singing and Scripture reading blend beautifully with the pastor's expositional message. Our hearts are edified and lifted toward God.

Working in and through the local church is a critical aspect of our spiritual exercise. The rest of the body of Christ needs our participation. There are also many opportunities in our neighborhoods to serve others. There are sick neighbors who need a visit and a helping hand. There are nursing homes and hospitals full of scared, lonely people. It is not hard to find people in need. Witnessing at home, at work, and as we go through our day is exercising our faith.

We are on the mission field wherever we go. Do not forget that Jesus said in Acts 1:8, "You shall be my witnesses..." Being a witness goes beyond merely witnessing with our mouths. Being a witness is about what you are, not just what you say. Francis of Assisi said "Preach the gospel at all times. If necessary, use words." Be all you should be for the Lord, and He will give you plenty of opportunities to say all you need to say.

**Good Growth in Grace (Sanctification)**

Everyone loves a baby. One of the most difficult things to do as a preacher is to get the attention of people in church who have a sweet little baby in front of them, turning around and smiling at them. Forget it. You have lost them. They are enamored by the little charmer. But no one wants to see that baby remain a baby. That is not normal or healthy. Likewise, there is something special and heart-warming about a newborn person in Christ. We patiently overlook their immature remarks and lack of Bible knowledge. But if that person perpetually stays a babe in Christ, there is something very unhealthy about their spiritual life. We are to "grow in grace and the knowledge of our Lord and Savior Jesus Christ" (1 Pet. 3:18).

**Good Rest (Trusting Faith)**

Perhaps you have heard or have read of stress being the silent killer. Stress, anxiety, worry, and fear can cause all types of illnesses—high blood pressure, insomnia, back pain, heart attacks, cancer, and depression being just a few. To have good health we need to have sufficient rest and even some time of relaxation.

I once came across a book that contained two side-by-side pictures of Abraham Lincoln. One was taken in 1861 just prior to the Civil War, and the other was taken in 1865 toward the end of the war. Just four years had transpired between the pictures, but Lincoln seemed to have aged drastically. Obviously, his face showed the results of those stressful years during the war.

While in Bible college, I was working a full-time job cooking at a restaurant from 10 p.m. to 6 a.m. I would come home from work, shower, and go to classes from 8 a.m. until 1:30 p.m. I would have meetings with my fellow ministry workers, eat lunch, study, and go to bed by 5 p.m. My wife would wake me at 9:30 p.m. to prepare to go to work again at 10 p.m. (I only lived four minutes from where I worked.) The weekends were even worse, because I served in a ministry in Chicago almost all day Saturday and Sunday.

To say the least, my wife and I lived on very little sleep. We were zealous in our faith but immature. Needless to say we became very ill and almost had to be hospitalized. Over the next year and a half Iris suffered two miscarriages and a multitude of other health issues, the effects of which were felt for years to come. Our bodies need adequate rest to function correctly. The Christian must learn to rest in the Lord. Philippians 4:6 says, "Be anxious for nothing." The word "anxious" means "to be pulled apart in different directions." There is no way of having a fruitful Christian walk without learning to rest in the Lord. Peter says to the believer "Casting all your care upon Him; for He careth for you" (1 Pet. 5:7). Psalm 37:7 says, "Rest in the Lord and wait patiently for him."

Are you getting the proper rest in Christ? The Bible says, "Trust in the Lord with all your heart; and lean not onto thine own understanding. In all thy ways acknowledge Him and He shall direct thy paths" (Prov. 3:5-6). Isaiah 57:20-21 says, "But the wicked are like the troubled sea, when it can not rest, whose waters cast up mire and dirt. There is no peace, saith my God, to the wicked."

## ’Tis So Sweet to Trust in Jesus

’Tis so sweet to trust in Jesus,
Just to take Him at His Word,
Just to rest upon His promise,
Just to know: “Thus saith the Lord.”

O how sweet to trust in Jesus,
Just to trust His cleansing Blood,
Just in simple faith to plunge me,
’Neath the healing, cleansing flood!

Yes, ’tis sweet to trust in Jesus,
Just from sin and self to cease,
Just from Jesus simply taking,
Life and rest, and joy and peace.

I’m so glad I learned to trust Thee,
Precious Jesus, Savior, Friend;
And I know that Thou art with me,
Wilt be with me to the end.

Jesus, Jesus, how I trust Him!
How I’ve proved Him o’er and o’er!
Jesus, Jesus, precious Jesus!
O for grace to trust Him more!

—Louisa M. R. Snead

# Autopsy Defined

Examine yourselves, whether ye be in the faith.—
2 Cor. 13:5

# Chapter 2

# Autopsy Defined

Webster's Dictionary defines autopsy as a "postmortem examination to determine cause of death." The word comes from two Greek words that mean "to look for yourself within" and "to see with your own eyes."

There are typically two types of autopsies. A forensic autopsy is the one that most people are aware of, because it is the kind that most of the popular TV shows feature. The forensic autopsy is performed to gather evidence to identify the cause of death, and whether the causes are accidental, intentional, or natural. If murder is suspected, then the perpetrator of the crime can sometimes be determined by examining the evidence acquired from this autopsy.

Recently, the body of a seventeen-year-old girl who was abducted a month earlier from her college campus was found in Virginia. As I'm writing this, the state is conducting an autopsy on her body. Through this forensic autopsy, the state seeks to gather evidence of how she was killed in hopes of determining who is responsible.

A second type of autopsy is a clinical autopsy. This can be done on almost anyone, regardless of the circumstances of the death. This autopsy is mainly a source of gathering important information to be used for educational purposes. These autopsies help train medical personnel and are essential in developing medicines and health habits that will sustain the lives of other people. Diseases and other health risks have been identified and, in some cases, eradicated altogether due to the information gleaned from clinical autopsies.

In this book, we will primarily be conducting a clinical autopsy. However, in chapters three and four we will closely analyze forensic evidence, because we will be dealing with a death as a result of a crime. The purpose of our autopsy of a dead church is to help keep us and our church from becoming spiritually dead. My desire is that we might learn from our mistakes and the mistakes of others. As the clinical autopsy of the dead can help maintain the well-being of the living, so may those who have failed spiritually help us to learn how we might avoid similar pitfalls.

This is a biblical technique of edification—teaching positive character traits from the failures of some well-known people in the Bible. Who has not learned from Adam and Eve's rebellion against God (Gen. 3:1-24)? Have we not been warned by Noah's becoming drunk with wine (Gen. 9:20)? Have we not only learned to walk by faith from Abraham but also of the consequences of having little faith (Gen. 12:1-20)? Is it virtue that we learn from Lot or the serious consequences of compromise (Gen. 19:12-38)? From David, while a man after God's own heart, do we not learn from the folly of lust and covetousness (2 Sam. 11:1-27; 12:1-23)? Then there is impetuous Peter who was so zealous for the Lord and yet eventually denied Him three times (Luke 22:54-62).

Indeed, there is much to be learned from the objective, clinical exposition of all such Scripture. The Bible is very clear that we are to examine ourselves to gauge our spiritual temperature (1 Cor. 11:28; 13:5). But the Bible also warns us in Jeremiah 17:9 that "the heart is deceitful above all things and desperately wicked: who can know it?" Only God can fully know our hearts. Jeremiah continues, "I, the Lord, search the heart, I try the reins [what is really inside you, which implies motives], even to give every man according to his ways, and according to the fruit of his doings" (Jer. 17:10). David pleaded with God, "Examine me, O Lord, and prove me; try my reins and my heart" (Ps. 26:2); "Search me, O God, and know my heart: try me, and know my thoughts: and see if there be any wicked way in me, and lead me in the way everlasting" (Ps. 139:23-24).

I am not interested in being the one to search you. I cannot even adequately search myself without the Lord's grace and power. If you are reading this book with an earnest desire to have God search you, please stop reading right now and bow your head and pray the scriptures I have just quoted. Ask God to search you and show you the issues of your heart. I hope you prayed that prayer. I have prayed that for myself many times, and I again prayed it just now. I also prayed for you, whoever you are, that you would be shown your heart by the One who alone can change you into His image!

We will now embark on our autopsy of a dead church. We have already defined autopsy as looking with our own eyes. We shall open up the body with the scalpel of God's two-edged sword, the Word of God—"For the word of God is quick [alive], and powerful, and sharper than any two-edged sword, piercing even to the dividing asunder [apart] of soul and spirit, and of the joints and marrow, and is a discerner of the thoughts and intents of the heart" (Heb. 4:12). Consider these words: "He that hath an ear, let him hear what the Spirit saith unto the churches" (Rev. 2:29; 3:6, 13, 22).

# Most Perfect Is the Law of God

Most perfect is the law of God,
Restoring those that stray;
His testimony is most sure,
Proclaiming wisdom's way.

The precepts of the Lord are right;
With joy they fill the heart;
The Lord's commandments all are pure,
And clearest light impart.

The fear of God is undefiled,
And ever shall endure;
The statutes of the Lord are truth,
And righteousness most pure.

The words which from my mouth proceed,
The thoughts within my heart,
Accept, O Lord, for Thou my Rock,
And my Redeemer art.

—From Psalm 119, The Psalter, 1912

# Traces of Adam's DNA

Wherefore, as by one man sin entered into the world, and death by sin; and so death passed upon all men, for that all have sinned.—Rom. 5:12

For as in Adam all die, even so in Christ shall all be made alive.—1 Cor. 15:22

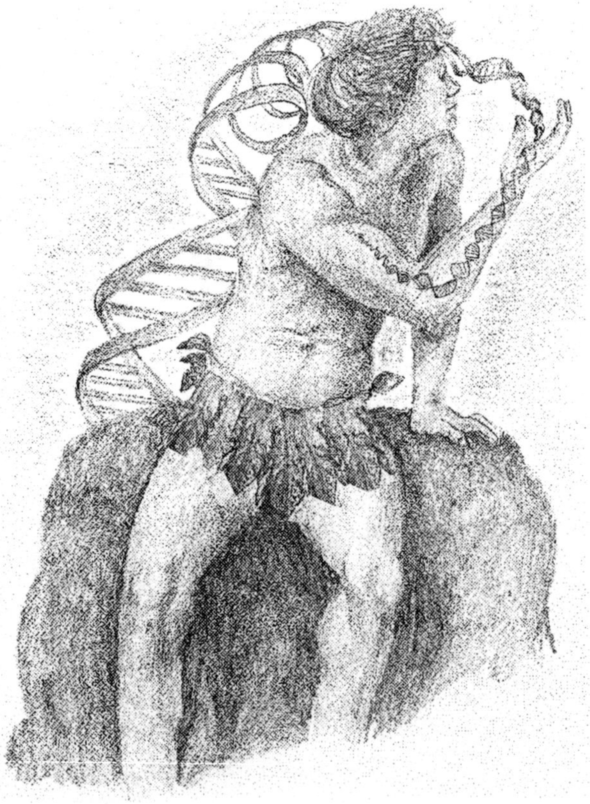

## Chapter 3

# Traces of Adam's DNA

Deoxyribonucleic acid, more commonly known as DNA, is the main constituent of the chromosomes of all organisms. DNA serves as the building block of every person's genetic makeup. It is DNA that distinguishes us from every other individual person and makes us unique. It is also used in determining the identity of a child's natural father. In the last twenty years, some murder cases have been solved by using just a minuscule amount of body fluid, skin tissue, or hair left behind by the suspect. When the DNA of these traces of evidence is compared with the suspect's DNA, it can link him or her to the crime scene.

As we begin the autopsy of a dead church we immediately find that DNA evidence links every person in that church with an infamous ancient crime. The crime scene is a garden named Eden. The lawbreakers are Adam and Eve. The offense is high treason against the Creator. Adam and Eve conspired with the archenemy of the Creator to rebel and to lead a whole race of people in mutiny against God. The consequences of the crime are that every person, as a descendant of this couple, has inherited their parents' rebellious nature toward the Creator; billions have died physically and spiritually. Testimony of this crime is found in Genesis 3.

The seeds of death are planted deep within the heart of every person in a church, including its beloved pastor. We are all sinners born into Adam's fallen race (Rom. 3:9-20). We are not just a little sick, but we are also dead in our trespasses and sins (Eph. 2:1, 5). This is not news to Bible-believing Christians. However, it is a doctrine that has been abandoned in its purest state by the liberal churches in America and is rarely taught, or even mentioned, in most evangelical churches today. If you watch a couple of the most popular preachers on TV today, you will not even hear the word sin.

The doctrine of original sin, the radical depravity of all people in Adam, is essential in dealing with the spiritual diseases and demise of the church. How can we find a cure when we are ignoring the root and seriousness of the problem? Putting a bandage on the forehead of someone with a brain tumor makes no sense and certainly does not cure anything. When I use the term radical depravity (some have used the term total depravity), I am not claiming we are as bad as we could be but that every area of our lives has been tainted by Adam's fallen nature. I use the word radical because it emphasizes the root or core of our being. The problem is a pervasive, sinful nature that touches our heart, mind, personality, emotions, conscience, motives, and will.

Recently, I took an undershirt out of my dresser drawer and found that it had just the slightest tinge of pink. On further investigation, I uncovered a pair of what were once white socks which also had a pink hue to them. To my dismay, I discovered several other items that had been thrown in the wash with a new red shirt. All of the clothes had fallen victim and were tainted, albeit to varying degrees of discoloration. Similarly, we, as Adam's race, have all been tainted by his fall.

**Why is this cardinal doctrine of the faith so important?**

First of all, the depravity of man is the clear teaching of Scripture (Genesis 3; Rom. 5:12-21; 1 Cor. 15:22-23). To deny this teaching is to deny the Word of God. Secondly, as proven from the texts above, to be wrong about the imputation (accrediting) of the Adam's sin to all mankind is to also be wrong about the imputation of Christ's sacrificial, atoning death for mankind. (Whether this atonement is particular or universal is beyond the scope of this book.) Adam's sin is imputed to us at our conception. Our sin is imputed to Christ in His atonement, or payment for sin, for us on the cross. Christ's righteousness (perfection) is imputed to all those who place their trust in

His death, burial, and resurrection. Each person who, by faith, has accepted the sacrificial work of Jesus Christ on the cross is declared justified (God declaring us guiltless) before God. This has always been the sound doctrine of the church. (If I have lost you with this doctrinal discussion, then Chapter 5 is important for you to read.)

Thirdly, if we fail to recognize that the lost people with whom we interact are spiritually dead and need to be regenerated (born from above), we may believe that our church programs will somehow win them for Christ. When we realize how the flesh will profit us nothing, then we will cast our hope on the Holy Spirit of God to bring new life to the lost (John 3:3-8). A church is measured by God not according to how many people are in the house of God but by how many people have Him dwelling in their heart. God does not take a head count, but He does take an account of the heart. I could take a corpse and place it in the middle of Disney World on the busiest day of the year, and that will not bring that corpse to life. Even so, I could place a spiritually dead person in a church with all the pomp and presentation, but if that person is not made alive by the Spirit, all is in vain.

Fourthly, the truth of the inherited sinfulness of man is important to remember while dealing with the church and her people. If we keep in mind this truth, we will not soon be shaken by disappointment when we see people acting out this fallen nature. I am not suggesting any excuses for sin; I merely advocate an understanding that all people will struggle with sin. The best of men are, at best, men. If you are waiting to find the perfect church full of perfect people, then you will never join any church.

The story is told of the man who was stranded alone on an island for three years. When he was finally found, the rescue workers noticed he had three structures built on the island. They asked him the purpose of each. He told them one building was his home. The second was his first church, which he no longer attended after being offended. The third building was the church he built after leaving his first church. I come across people who have been hurt or offended by someone at church and have become greatly disillusioned. Some of these people have abandoned church completely. Mark it down: you will be hurt and sometimes offended! It goes with the territory of being a fallen person in a world full of fallen people.

I played quarterback on my high school and college football teams. This was before they instituted all these rules in an effort to protect the quarterback from unnecessary roughness. Many times, I would get hit as I was throwing the ball but was able to brace myself because I could see the impact coming. Several times, however, I did not see the opposing player coming because he was approaching me from behind (what is commonly called the blindside). These hits were always much more devastating and more often caused injury. (That is why a right-handed quarterback will usually have his best offensive lineman to his left, which is his most vulnerable side or his blindside, while he is throwing the ball.) The Lord does not want us to be blindsided because of our ignorance of this or any biblical truth. It may hurt us, but we do not need to be totally demoralized when we see people express their sinful nature.

**Why have so many churches fallen away from this important doctrine of the faith?**

First of all, there are too many churches that no longer believe the first eleven chapters of Genesis as being literally true. They no longer believe creation as it is set forth in Genesis 1 and 2. They no longer see man as separate and above the animal kingdom made in the image of God. The concept of a literal Adam and Eve has been replaced by evolution. The authority of God, as our Creator, to command and to guide us has been eroded. Even the concept of marriage as designed by God is passé. Without a real Adam and Eve as the head of mankind, there is no real fall of man by original sin. This is important to remember while trying to win people to Christ in post-Christian America. We have a whole generation that has no concept of the reality of their rebellion against a Creator that they have been told does not exist.

Modern man is looking for human identity in a past of nothingness and in a future of nothingness. He has been told that he is a product of chance and is really only a grown-up germ. I am convinced we are dealing with a generation of people in America who believe the cross of Christ is foolishness because they, like the ancient Greeks (1 Cor. 1:23), have believed in manmade myths to explain their origins and destiny. Many churches have turned their backs on creation and the Creator. Churches need to return to teaching the Bible truth of a literal creation and a literal Adam and Eve! This will establish the authority of the Creator and the rebellion of the creatures, and eventually bring people to the necessity of the cross of Christ.

The Bible does not drop the gospel of Jesus Christ and His work on the cross into a vacuum, detached from thousands of years of human history. Man's history is truly His-story (God's) and is inextricably woven into God's eternal redemptive plan. The next domino to fall is the veracity of the Word of God. It is directly and indirectly assailed in the minds of the people who attend these churches. If there is no trustworthy Bible, then there is no creation, no fall of man, no sin, no judgment, no hell, no salvation, no heaven. Some churches want to dwell on heaven to the exclusion of the rest of these truths. God's truth is not a bus that we can hop on at any point and jump off when we don't like where it is taking us. It is more like an airplane. We get on at Genesis 1:1 and we have to trust the pilot (God) to safely guide us to our destination at Revelation 22:21.

Another reason some churches are not teaching and preaching this truth is that it is not positive or popular. No one wants to dwell on the fact that we are all sinners at heart. We would rather fill people's heads with self-help psychology and feel-good pep rallies. There is a plethora of churches, books, CDs, television shows, and radio programs that are all vying for the consumer's purse. Rick Warren, in his book The Purpose Driven Church, certainly is on target when he challenges the church to be correctly motivated by eternal truths. However, too many churches are consumer-driven and pragmatically adapting the church to a "whatever works" mentality. Telling people who are lost and self-centered that they are born sinners is not very popular. People can just go down the street to the more sensitive, smooth-talking Reverend Sugar-Sweet Speaker or tune into his cousin Reverend Edward Ear-Tickler on television. Consider this quote from author and speaker Charles Colson: "This myth [that man is basically good] deludes people into thinking that they are always victims, never villains; always deprived, never depraved. It dismisses responsibility as the teaching of a darker age. It can excuse any crime, because it can always blame something else—a sickness of our society or a sickness of the mind. One writer called the modern age "the golden age of exoneration." When guilt is dismissed as the illusion of narrow minds, then no one is accountable, even to his conscience. The irony is that this should come alive in this century, of all centuries, with the gulags and death camps and killing fields. G.K. Chesterton once said, "The doctrine of original sin is the only philosophy empirically validated by centuries of recorded human history."

As preachers and pastors, we must be faithful to the truth. We must be the way Faithful and Christian were in John Bunyan's allegorical classic of the Christian life, Pilgrim's Progress. Christian and Faithful were fellow pilgrims traveling to the Celestial City (heaven), and the path to the city led them through the wicked and worldly town of Vanity Fair. As they traveled along, each merchant of the world's goods tried to lure them with their wares. The pilgrims turned to the unholy solicitors and declared as they pushed them aside, "We buy the truth and sell it not" (Prov. 23:23). Unfortunately, too often today the truth is freely traded for lies.

I have a friend named Josef Tson from Romania. He grew up under the oppression of the communist regime. He has been arrested several times for preaching the Word of God. After being threatened several times, he was exiled from Romania because the communists did not want to turn him into a martyr. Josef went to England in the 1970s and studied at Cambridge. He was mentored for a season under the esteemed Dr. Martyn Lloyd-Jones, pastor at Westminster Chapel for thirty years.

While Josef was studying for his doctorate, he began making plans to return to his beloved Romania to train younger men for the ministry. He told me that many of the other young men studying there with him from England and the United States could not understand why he wanted to go back to Romania. They would say to him, "How do you think you can be successful in that land under such atheistic persecution?" Josef looked at me, shook his head, and said, "How very western and wrong in thinking. God has not called me to be successful. God has called me to be faithful."

My plea to the churches is to not neglect the doctrines of man's fallen nature in Adam and his salvation in Christ alone. Return to the literal creation as depicted in Genesis 1–3. Mine is the same plea that the Lord of the church had for the dead church of Sardis. Wake up! Repent! Remember these truths that are foundational to your faith and apply them to your life and that of your church.

# And Can It Be That I Should Gain?

And can it be that I should gain,
An interest in the Savior's blood?
Died He for me, who caused His pain?
For me, who Him to death pursued?
Amazing Love! How can it be,
That Thou, my God, shouldst die for me?

He left His Father's throne above,
So free, so infinite His grace;
Emptied Himself of all but love,
And bled for Adam's helpless race;
'Tis mercy all, immense and free;
For, O my God, it found out me.

Long my imprisoned spirit lay,
Fast bound in sin and nature's night;
Thine eye diffused a quick'ning ray,
I woke, the dungeon flamed with light;
My chains fell off, my heart was free;
I rose, went forth, and followed Thee.

Amazing love! How can it be,
That Thou my God, shouldst die for me?

—Charles Wesley

# Fingerprints of the Murderer

Ye are of your father the devil, and the lusts (desires) of your father ye will do. He was a murderer from the beginning, and abode not in the truth, because there is no truth in him. When he speaketh a lie, he speaketh of his own (his native language is lying): for he is a liar, and the father of it.—John 8:44

# Chapter 4

# Fingerprints of the Murderer

Although man has been aware that fingerprints can identify a person since ancient Babylon and China, it is only within the last hundred years that fingerprints have been used effectively for capturing criminals. Archeologists have discovered thumbprints on clay tablets related to business transactions dated millennia ago. However, it was not until the year 1924 that the FBI started using fingerprints as part of its Identification Division. No two people in all the world have identical fingerprints. As a matter of fact, no two digits belonging to the same person have the same fingerprint.

As we conduct the autopsy of this dead church, we will find the fingerprints of the devil all over the body of Christ. We must look carefully, for it is commonly known that it takes great patience and skill to get a good set of fingerprints off the skin of a corpse. We are also aware that Satan is very sly and subtle, attempting to go undetected as he works his evil schemes. Just as each fingerprint has a series of ridges, lines, and loops that together create a unique pattern identified as only that person's print, Satan has some identifying traits that can tell us of his wicked work going on in a church, a family, or an individual life. To identify these traits, we will examine his personality, position, power, practices, and ultimate purpose.

First, we must be conscious of that fact that Satan is real today. People are either ignorant of that fact or indifferent to it. He is blinding the unsaved (2 Cor. 4:4) and beguiling the saved (2 Cor.

11:3). People doubt his existence and are unaware of his power. We do not want Satan to get an advantage over us because we are ignorant of his well thought-out plans and devices (2 Cor. 2:11). The Bible tells us his plan is to destroy us. Peter warns us, "Be sober, be vigilant; because your adversary the devil, as a roaring lion, walketh about, seeking whom he may devour" (1 Pet. 5:8).

**His Personality**

He is proud. Isaiah 14:12-17 and Ezekiel 28:12-17 tell us the combined story of how Lucifer was created a beautiful, anointed cherub long before the creation of the earth as we know it today. He had access to the presence of God. He was adorned with the most radiant precious stones and had pipes that were probably the source of the most sublime music. God had set him in a very high and exalted position. He was likely one of three archangels, along with Michael and Gabriel.

Yet, all this was not enough for Lucifer. His beauty caused him to be lifted up in his heart. He said in his heart that he would ascend above all the other stars and beings. He would exalt his throne above all others so as to be like God. Five times he used the word "I," indicating his pride and his desire to be ruler of his own life without the restrictions of God.

Lucifer the archangel became Satan the archenemy of God and was cast out of heaven. He would later come to Adam and Eve with that same proud boast that you can be as God (Genesis 3). Pride is a core sin that people in every church struggle with. The pastor can become proud and lifted up in his position. He is tempted to lord it over the people of God. Peter warns pastors of this (1 Pet. 5:3, 5-6) and encourages humility, because God resists the proud. Power is often linked with pride. Some very wealthy people are never satisfied, because it is not more money they seek but rather more power. Some people in the church desire to be noticed by others and want the choir positions, solo opportunities, deacon's positions, Sunday school teachers, or Adult Bible Fellowship leaders.

The occasions are endless for pride to overtake us. Pride is a key weapon in Satan's arsenal against the church. Even if you are part of an excellent church, you can be overtaken with pride about your church.

Pride will keep many people from seeing their weaknesses and repenting of their failures. Study what the book of Proverbs has to say about pride and haughtiness. It challenges us all. Take a reflective look at so much of what is promoted by television ministries. Not all, but many of these shows have people strutting back and forth with a haughty countenance. They demand things from the Holy God of the universe as though He were their waiter or bellhop.

Some of the reformers, like Martin Luther, decided to make comic caricatures of Satan because they thought that with his pride it might demoralize him. Unfortunately, it led to the depictions of Satan as an absurd, silly creature with red tights, horns, and a pitchfork. He is a far more formidable and fierce enemy. He has subtly manipulated this image to his advantage and has deceived the church about his true nature.

**His Position**

He is the prince of this evil world system (John 12:31). Evil men are his puppets. Dictators and many world leaders are under his limited dominion. He is behind every governmental decree that attacks and persecutes the church (Ezekiel 28; Daniel 10). He is a ruler of his own kingdom (Matt. 12:26). All the evil men and spirits are controlled by him. There may not always be a manmade conspiracy against the work of the Bible-preaching church, but you can be sure there is an ongoing spiritual conspiracy led by Satan and his subordinates. His is the unseen hand manipulating evil men.

He is a prince of the power of the air (Eph. 2:2).This is commonly considered to mean evil spirits. I was in a meeting in Malawi, Africa, when a possessed woman starting screaming obscenities in English, a language she had never spoken before. She cursed Christ and all His servants. I was present when the pastor and deacons later took her to her home and prayed for her for almost an hour. Before we left she was sitting up, in her right mind, praising the Lord Jesus Christ, and calling Him Savior.

I know this seems corny and unbelievable to many Americans, but Satan is real and working in our churches through evil spirits, causing much disruption. He is oppressing many people in the body of Christ. We wrestle not with flesh and blood, but we are engaged in spiritual warfare (Eph. 6:12). He is the ruler of his own angels (Matt. 25:41). These are a third of the angelic host that was cast out of heaven, along with Satan, when they rebelled against the Almighty. These angels of darkness do Satan's bidding and are the enemies of God's church and God's people.

Satan is called the god of this world (2 Cor. 4:4). Satan has his own false religion. He is the greatest counterfeiter the world has even known. He has a false gospel (Gal.1:6-10). He has seducing spirits and doctrine of devils (1 Tim. 4:1). He even has a cup and table of demons (1 Cor. 10:20-21) in the place of the Lord's Supper. The true church is called the bride of Christ, but in the end times the Antichrist will control the great harlot, the false church, which is Satan's bride (Revelation 17). Satan continues to seed the true church with false prophets and deceitful workers. His ministers disguise themselves as righteous doers of good. Satan even presents himself as an angel of light (2 Cor. 11:13-14). Not everything that glitters is gold! Not everybody who is talking about God is of God!

It was a bitter cold January afternoon in 1988. I was serving as the associate pastor of Calvary Chapel Church of Staten Island, New York. The mother of a faithful family that attended our church called me at my home. She was crying and asked if I might go see her daughter, who was addicted to heroin. Her daughter had contracted AIDS and was living on the streets. After I asked several questions as to where she might be, I set out to find her.

Having done door-to-door visitation over most of northern Staten Island, I knew of a couple of crack houses in that neighborhood. I found her sitting on the front steps of the second house I visited. She was in bad shape, but she recognized me from seeing me at her family's home in the past. I helped her to my car. She refused to let me take her back to her mother's home. I was aware of a decent homeless shelter set up in a church several blocks away. She agreed to let me take her there. I drove up to the shelter and helped her inside. We were greeted immediately by a tall, well-dressed, and soft-spoken man. He introduced himself as Bob Lord and invited us in. He quickly motioned for a woman to escort the young lady to a table where some hot coffee and food were set before her.

In the meantime Mr. Lord directed me to his small office and took a little information. He told me that he was also a man of God. He took my phone number so he could keep me informed about how the woman was doing. I was so impressed by Mr. Lord's willingness to help. He was well-spoken, intelligent, and congenial. After saying goodnight to the young woman and Mr. Lord, I went home. A week later I received a follow-up call from Bob Lord asking how that young woman was doing, for he had not seen her for three days. I told him she was preparing to go away to a Christian rehab camp in a distant state. He said, "Praise the Lord!" Again, I was impressed by this man's kind consideration.

On Feb. 7, 1988, America's Most Wanted aired its first show and featured an escaped criminal who had murdered a husband and wife, along with their baby. While he was out on bail awaiting his trial for those crimes, he kidnapped and raped a woman. He locked her in the trunk of her car. He took her infant son and callously tossed him on the side of the road to die of exposure. He was caught and found guilty of all these crimes and had been serving several consecutive life sentences when he managed to escape.

His name was David James Roberts, but I knew him as none other than Bob Lord. You can imagine my shock when I saw his picture all over the news as the first criminal caught via America's Most Wanted television program. One of the first thoughts I had was, "No marvel, for Satan himself is transformed into an angel of light. Therefore it is no great thing if his ministers also are transformed as the ministers of righteousness" (2 Cor. 11:14-15).

**His Power**

He has the power of darkness, which blinds people from truth (Col. 1:13). He has the power of death, which causes people to fear (Heb. 2:14). However, the power of death is limited by God's will (Job 2:6), and that power is swallowed up in victory for the Christian because of the death and resurrection of Jesus Christ (1 Cor. 15:54). He has, and will have in the end-times, the power of signs and lying wonders (2 Thess. 2:9). Not every supernatural act is of God or is what it appears to be. The power of Satan is not anything to be scoffed at, for even Michael the archangel calls on the sovereign power of God Almighty in order to rebuke Satan (Jude 9).

**His Practices**

In the original temptation of Adam and Eve (Genesis 3) we see Satan's mode of operation. He uses the opposite of faith—*doubt.* Here is the first question in the Bible, and it is Satan placing doubt in the minds of Adam and Eve about the Word of God: "Hath God said…?" He then uses *deception*: "You shall not surely die." This is an outright lie.

Next Satan brings *division.* After Adam and Eve ate of the fruit they died spiritually, which separated them from God. When God confronts them for rebelliously eating the fruit, Eve blames the serpent, and Adam blames Eve. When Adam blames Eve, he indirectly blames God for being the one that gave him Eve.

Satan is continually seeking to divide us from God and each other. When people in church are playing the blame game, you can be sure the devil is at work. Satan amuses us with the delights of sin. He then confuses us about what God has said about sin. He excuses us to participate in sin (Gen. 3:1-6). Finally, he will be there to accuse us of our willingness to sin (Rev. 12:10). Think about it and take heed of his attacks on you and your church. Satan brings *death* and *destruction.* After Adam and Eve gave into his temptation, they died spiritually, and physical death came into the world. Death became part of life for everyone who would follow. The process of decay began, and we see it everywhere around us to this day. Satan cannot get his hands on God to kill Him, so he is dedicated to destroying the life of every person, because we are made in the image of God.

**Satan's Ultimate Purpose**

The summation of all of Satan's practices is the defaming and dethroning of God in the hearts of all people. He was not able to actually usurp God's throne as he desired. His second plan of attack is to discredit God and keep Him from being enthroned in the hearts of men, women, and children. He does this with the lost by seeking to keep them blinded from the truth of the gospel. He also seeks to distract the saved from focusing on God. A dead or dying church will be very man-centered with emphasis on the desires of man rather than the worship of God. Man becomes the measure of all things. Oh yes, there may even be a crowd of people, but they are not lifting up the Lord of the Bible. They have a god made in the image of man (Rom. 1:18-25), and that suits Satan's purposes just fine.

Examine with me the saga of Job. God points out Job's exemplary life to Satan. Satan in turn accuses Job of loving and obeying God only because God has been so generous to Job. Indirectly, of course, Satan is saying that God can only get people to love Him if He bribes them. Satan is not only accusing Job of insincere worship, but he is also backhanding the Lord about His worthiness of worship. Imagine one man saying to another, "Your wife only married you and stays married to you because of the money you give her." That is not only insulting to the wife but also very insulting to the husband's worth as a man.

As the story unfolds, God allows Satan to take everything from Job. All his earthly goods are stolen or destroyed, and all ten of his beloved children are killed. Then God allows Satan to attack the body of Job with horrible sickness. Even Job's wife becomes an instrument of Satan when she encourages Job to curse God and die. Job does not heed her advice but rather rebukes her and worships God. Satan's accusations were found to be a lie. Satan could not remove God from His throne in the heart of Job, and Job demonstrated that God is worthy to be served no matter the circumstances.

The latent fingerprints of Satan can be seen all over many churches today that have overemphasized the health-and-wealth mentality. By wrongly asserting that God always wants to give us everything we desire in the way of wealth and well-being, we are setting people up to believe Satan's lie. "If God really loved you, you would never be sick or financially challenged," some say. Millions are falling into that trap and end up worshiping a false god. Those who happen to have wealth and good health focus more on the gift than the Giver. They are candidates for a proud heart because their faith is the reason, so they have been told, that God has blessed them. And those who, through whatever the circumstances of life (they are told it is their lack of faith), suffer setbacks in their lives become very disillusioned with God. Both of these scenarios dishonor God and help fulfill the ultimate purpose of Satan.

Please don't misunderstand what I am saying. I believe God can and does heal people and does bless people with material wealth, but it is not my birthright as a Christian to have all these things now. Many times God chooses to glorify His name in us and through us by allowing our suffering. The whole volume of *Foxe's Book of Martyrs* gives witness to this.

How is it that we know Jim Elliot? Do we know him for the BMW he drove or the lavish house he owned? Or was it his excellent health and wavy hair? Do we remember Jim Elliot for his thousand-dollar designer suits or crystal cathedral? Or do we know him because of his national television show? No. We know him for the suffering and death he endured at the hands of the Auca Indians, the very people he sought to win for Christ. "[He makes] His ministers a flame of fire," Elliot wrote while a student at Wheaton College. "Am I ignitable? God deliver me from the dread asbestos of 'other things.' Saturate me with the oil of the Spirit that I may be aflame. But flame is transient, often short-lived. Canst thou bear this my soul—short life? In me there dwells the spirit of the Great Short-Lived, whose zeal for God's house consumed Him."

Can we pray such a prayer? The apostle Paul did (2 Cor. 12:7-10). I fear that Satan has bewitched many folks in the church with the "asbestos of other things," such as health, wealth, celebrity, and comfort. Are we willing to serve a God who is worthy of our worship and love simply because of who He is? Tertullian said more than eighteen hundred years ago, "The blood of the martyrs is the seed of the church." Notice he did not say their wealth and health. If we can pray such a prayer, we can expose the lie of the devil and bring glory to God!

**Our Power**

The church and her people must realize that we cannot stand alone, without the Lord. We are to be strong in the Lord and the power of His might and put on the whole armor of God (Eph. 6:10-18). We must be girded with the truth against the father of lies. The breastplate of righteousness gives us the position of being right with God because of what Jesus did for us on the cross. It gives us the practical benefit of knowing we are living in honor of God. When we are not living right before God we are attacked outwardly by unbelievers as hypocrites. We are attacked inwardly by our conscience (Prov. 28:1). We are attacked by the accuser of the brethren, Satan (Rev. 12:10).

We must remember with confidence that we have peace with God through the gospel of Jesus Christ. This gives us sure footing. The fiery darts of the devil are his lies to tempt us to disobey God's commands. The shield of faith helps us reject these lustful temptations. The helmet of salvation gives us assurance of our salvation to stand against Satan's doubts and discouragement. And the sword of the Spirit is the soldier's only weapon. It is the Word of God, and with this the Christian is able to defensively ward off the blows of the enemy and destroy the strategies of Satan (Matt. 4:4-11). We are not to believe every spirit, but we are to try every spirit to see if it is of God. God warns us that there are many false prophets (1 John 4:1).

**Our Position**

"Greater is He who is in you than he that is in the world," according to 1 John 4:4. We are adopted into God's family by the work of our older brother, Jesus Christ, and are accepted in the Beloved (Eph. 1:3-6). God is for us, and nothing and no one can be against us. We are more than conquerors through Him who loved us, and nothing shall separate us from the love of God (Rom. 8:31-39). We are His sheep in the hand of the Shepherd, and no one can pluck us out of His hand (John 10:26-30).

## A Mighty Fortress Is Our God

A mighty fortress is our God,
A bulwark never failing;
Our helper He, amid the flood,
Of mortal ills prevailing
For still our ancient foe,
Doth seek to work us woe;
His craft and power are great,
And, armed with cruel hate,
On earth is not his equal.

Did we in our own strength confide,
Our striving would be losing;
Were not the right Man on our side,
The Man of God's own choosing.
Dost ask who that may be?
Christ Jesus, it is He;
Lord Sabaoth is His name,
From age to age the same,
And He must win the battle.

And tho' this world, with devils filled,
Should threaten to undo us;
We will not fear, for God hath willed
His truth to triumph through us.
The prince of darkness grim—
We tremble not for him;
His rage we can endure,
For lo! His doom is sure,
One little word shall fell him.

That Word above all earthly powers—
No thanks to them-abideth:
The Spirit and the gifts are ours,
Through Him who with us sideth.
Let goods and kindred go,
This mortal life also;
The body they may kill:
God's truth abideth still,
His kingdom is forever.

—Martin Luther

# Mindless Christianity

And be not conformed to this world: but be ye transformed by the renewing of your mind, that ye may prove what is that good, and acceptable, and perfect will of God.—Rom. 12:2

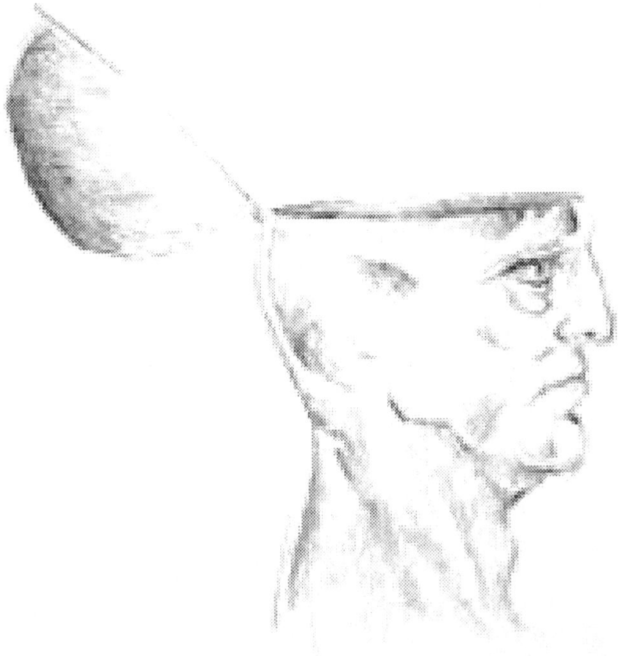

# Chapter 5

# Mindless Christianity

We now move to the examination of the brain, which is actually the organ that houses the mind. In about 450 B.C. the Greek physician Alcmaeon was the first to use anatomic dissection of animals as a basis for his theories. He concluded from his studies that the brain, not the heart, is the central organ of sensation and thought. This idea directly contradicted the accepted theory of his time, which held that the heart was the true seat of intelligence.

We all know today that the mind is the gateway to the heart. If we are to reach into the sanctuary of a person's heart (seat of the emotions, desires, and affections) we must pass through the vestibule of their mind. It sounds trite, but our thoughts are truly the blueprints to our actions.

The dead church has had real brain damage. In some cases an enchanting or forceful preacher has performed a 'spiritual lobotomy', hindering any deep and independent biblical thinking on the part of the people of the church. Any true scriptural discernment is usually squashed as "a critical spirit" and subtly, or not so subtly, discredited from the bully pulpit.

"I believe a very large majority of churchgoers are merely unthinking, slumbering worshipers of an unknown God," said Charles H. Spurgeon. Spurgeon was once rebuked by a woman who told him that "God does not need our education," to which he quipped, "You are correct, madam, but neither does He need our ignorance." We desperately need to think and act biblically.

The mind plays a crucial part in the health of a Christian and a church. We are not to worship the mind, but neither are we to waste it. The culture in which we live is immersed in amusement. The amusement industry is a powerful influence even on the church. The very word "amuse" means "the absence of thought." This is a trap of Satan to discourage the development of discerning and critical thinking skills of the people of God.

We are to take every thought into the obedience of Christ (2 Cor. 10:5). We are to be noble as the Bereans were and filter all that comes our way through the lie detector of the Word of God (Acts 17:11). I have actually sat in a church service where the pastor discouraged us from having our Bibles open before us as he, the preacher, was speaking. Any critique of this man's messages was met with fierce personal attacks on the motives of the person who dared to speak up. And there was always the standard of "might makes right." His supporters pragmatically proclaim, "Look how big this man's ministry is! He must be right!" They offer no real biblical verification for his teaching. At best, they simply present more perverted twisting of the Scripture.

We are repeatedly warned in the Bible not to fulfill the lust of the flesh or of the mind (Eph. 2:3). "What the country needs is dirtier fingernails and cleaner minds," said humorist Will Rogers. We are not to walk as the rest of the world walks, after the vanity of their minds (Eph. 4:17). We are not to emulate the enemies of Christ. Their end is destruction, and their belly (the dietary laws of the Judaizers) is their god. They mind earthly things, preoccupied with physical ceremonies and rituals (Phil. 3:19). We are warned about unbelief potentially defiling our conscience and mind (Titus 1:15). Peter admonishes us to gird up the loins of our minds—or pull up the loose ends of sloppy thinking—and focus on the grace of the cross of Jesus Christ (1 Pet. 1:13).

The dead and dying churches of America have generally been devolving into an amusement park atmosphere. Oh, sure, some of the bigger churches have the money to be more like Disney World, and at the smaller churches you have to settle for the county fair, but all the rides basically go around and around and up and down. You get off where you got on, only a little shakier and a lot dizzier. Much effort is put into winning prizes that are not worth the time, effort, and money that people spend attempting to acquire them, and the only true goal in many cases is to impress someone like a child, a girlfriend, or spouse.

I like to refer to this as 'cotton candy' Christianity. It has no real substance. Part of its allure is the carnival atmosphere that helps sell it to you. It is made of air and colored sugar. It leaves you all sticky and full of empty calories. It holds far more promise to the eyes than it delivers nourishment to the body. Sounds like the entertainment-driven churches of our age. Some of these churches have too much hype and too little lasting spiritual substance.

**The World Conforms and the Word Transforms the Mind**

I would like to use Roman 12:2 as a launching pad to look at the some temptations to conform our minds to this world. Conforming refers to that which applies pressure from without. It presses us into the world's mold. In turn, we will look at the tool that transforms our minds and directs our wills to know and do God's will. Transformation is that which happens from the inside out.

The context of Romans 12:2 is obviously the previous eleven chapters of Romans, in which the apostle Paul has laid out in linear logic the reasonableness of our surrender and service to God. After he has systematically confirmed the helplessness and hopelessness of all mankind as sinners, he gloriously directs our attention to the seeking grace and love of the sovereign God of the universe. This love sought us and bought us even while we were yet in our sins. This love has, sacrificially through Christ, given us peace and joy while allowing no condemnation! This gracious love makes everything work together for our good and causes us to look more like Jesus all the time. This love will never, never, no never, leave us or let us go! Finally, Paul cannot contain himself any longer but breaks out into a doxology about the depth of God's wisdom and knowledge. He is overwhelmed with our inability to completely absorb and understand God's marvelous ways. Paul simply reposes in the person and glory of God Almighty (Rom. 11:33-36).

Therefore, Paul continues in Chapter 12, is it not just our reasonable and logical (both words related to the mind) response to these truths to simply surrender our total being to our gracious, loving and all powerful God in service? Theologian and writer J. I. Packer says, "The secular world never understands Christian motivation....From the plan of salvation I learn that the true driving force in authentic Christian living is, and ever must be, not the hope of gain, but the heart of gratitude." It is logical because of all Christ has done for us. It is logical because of what He continues to do for us. It is logical because it is God's will, and that will is good, pleasing, and perfect. Finally, it is logical because only spiritual things will last, and therefore they are the best investments for us as Christians. Elementary economics tells us that it is not wise to invest too much in consumable goods. The will of God is eternal.

### The Attacks of the "Isms": Viruses that Seek to Conform Our Minds

What are some of the temptations to conform to the world's philosophies? It is important that worldliness be defined in the context of this text. Paul is speaking about our minds and how we think, not so much about how we behave—though, granted, right thinking produces right behavior. But here Paul is dealing with the inside-out issues that each believer is dealing with while in this present age. Ideas rule and reign in the hearts of people, and they gain their access through the mind. They are like a virus that enters the body and infects it. There may be only a low-grade fever at first, but later as the sickness spreads, the temperature rises and can eventually kill the body. The corpse of this dead church has the signs of a viral infection in the mind caused by certain "isms," philosophies of life.

### Secularism

This is a worldview that states that all there is to the universe is what we can see, feel, touch, weigh, and measure. It is the here and now apart from the eternal. Carl Sagan, on his television series Cosmos, put it this way: "The cosmos is all that is or ever was or ever will be." That is secularism with an attitude. (Sagan died a few years ago, and I am confident that his worldview has changed drastically.) There is no access to anything beyond this world, here and now. Solomon called it "the vanity of life under the sun" in the book of Ecclesiastes. We must no longer accept this worldview of living just for the here and now, but as Christians our minds must be renewed with eternal values. Does the church budget reflect eternal values, such as souls, or earthly values, like buildings?

**Humanism**

This is another philosophy that the renewed mind of the Christian must reject. Humanism is not to be confused with the very noble efforts of humanitarianism, which seeks to help our fellow humans in need. Humanism makes man the measure of all things. Man controls his own destiny. Man is his own god. There are many churches that have taken steps in this direction by making man the center of church programs. Man and his felt needs are the driving forces of these churches. They would certainly deny this subtle shift toward humanism, and I believe they are sincere in their denials.

In most cases, I am not impugning anyone's motives; I am convinced these churches are doing what they believe is correct. But I am asking all of us to examine closely the Word of God. God's glory should be the focal point, not our creature comforts or manmade goals, and certainly not our egos. Daniel 4 reminds us that God would not tolerate the humanistic arrogance of Nebuchadnezzar, the king of Babylon. The king looked out over of the great city of ancient Babylon and basically declared that all he saw was of him, by him, and for the glory of his majesty. Sometime thereafter, God struck him down to live as an animal for seven years.

Humanism is very deceiving. It does not really elevate man to a god but rather devalues man to his most basic instincts. God's truth elevates man to his real status as the crown of His creation, made in the image of God with capacities of reason far beyond the rest of God's creation. Notice in Daniel 4:34-37 how the king's reason and sanity returns to him at the same moment his humility before God is manifested. "I…lifted up mine eyes to heaven, and mine understanding returned unto me, and I blessed the Most High, and I praised and honored Him that liveth forever, whose dominion is an everlasting dominion, and His kingdom is from generation: and all the inhabitants of the earth are reputed as nothing: and he doeth according to His will in the army of heaven, and among the inhabitants of the earth: and none can stay His hand, or say unto Him, What doest thou?"

Another dangerous step toward humanism is the efforts of churches to return God's favor by creating God in the image of man. Romans 1:21-25 warns us of a people who do not like the God portrayed in the Bible, and so they seek to remake God in their own imaginations. They design a corruptible god who is more like the creature than the Creator. Churches are doing this by teaching that God is limited in what He knows (a recent heresy called "open theism" has sprung out of this). They say God does not know the future or, more subtly, the future is out of His control. Man, and his will, ultimately controls the destiny of the planet, so they say.

Still other churches deem God sovereign in some passing areas of life but not in the eternal destiny of the souls of men. Oh, they will never admit such an assessment of their doctrine, but the god they worship is not the Almighty but the "almost-mighty." No church or Christian will ever rise above their concept of God. A. W. Tozer said it this way, "Let us beware lest we in our pride accept the erroneous notion that idolatry consist only in the kneeling before visible objects of adoration, and that civilized people are therefore free from it. The essence of idolatry is the entertainment of thoughts about God that are unworthy of Him. It begins in the mind and may be present where no overt act of worship has taken place." When was the last time your church did a study on the person and attributes of the God of the Bible? Remember this truth—manmade religions are not men seeking God. Manmade religions are men seeking to flee the God of the Bible by making gods in the own image (Rom. 1:18-23). These are the seed thoughts of humanism.

**Narcissism**

This is one of the philosophies Paul warns Timothy about regarding the last days: "lovers of their own selves" (2 Tim. 3:1). This is a term that speaks of an abnormal love of self. The term comes from the Greek myth about a young man, Narcissus, who was considered the most handsome of all men. One day he looked into a pool of water and saw his own reflection. He then fell hopelessly in love with himself and was basically useless from then on. This is the world we live in today, and this virus has infected the church. Most people join a church for what they can get out of it rather than how they might serve through it. These people come into the fellowship with the mindset, "Here I am!" The Christ-like attitude towards others should be, "Oh, there you are!" However, churches market their programs to mirror McDonald's, "You deserve a break today!" or Burger King's "Have it your way!" It is no wonder congregations are not looking for humble, godly men as pastors anymore. They want professional CEOs with Madison Ave techniques. The church is called to minister to this world's people—not to manipulate them for our purposes.

**Hedonism**

This philosophy says pleasure is the chief end of man. Paul warns Timothy that in the last days, people will be "lovers of pleasures more than lovers of God" (2 Tim. 3:4). We know this is what the world promotes, but in this context Paul is warning that this attitude will seep into the church. He identifies them as people who have a form of godliness (2 Tim. 3:5). These texts are an open rebuke to many of our churches and Christians today. For example, many use the Lord's Day as their day to play rather than worship the Lord.

**Relativism**

This philosophy states that there is no absolute truth. What is truth for you is not necessarily truth for me. A person's perspective is all that matters. Again, most evangelical churches would adamantly proclaim their position against relativism. We all beat our chest and stand unflinchingly for the Bible and its claim as absolute truth. However, as a practical matter, most of our church people are so poorly taught and uneducated in what the Bible teaches that they become unwilling participants in relativism. It is the essence of arrogance for a believer to proclaim they believe something just because they believe it without any objective Biblical foundation.

I was approached by a woman who visited our church years ago. She gave me a tape of a preacher she had recently heard and really enjoyed. As I listened to this man teach on the resurrection of Christ, I realized he did not believe in the literal bodily resurrection of Christ. It was all a spiritual event. I later questioned her about this truth, and she brushed me off as "picking on him and being jealous of his eloquence," as she saw it. Well, he was eloquent—wrong, but he was good at being wrong, as was Satan in Genesis 3. He lied, but he was a smooth talker. She saw it as my opinion against his and that was that, as far as she was concerned. At that moment she was embracing relativism in a very practical sense. Some Christians are not diligent enough to learn their Bibles, and when an issue arises they would rather just deem it unimportant and a matter of personal preference. We are not discussing carpet color or paving a parking lot, but we are talking about eternal matters that will determine people's eternal destiny.

**Pluralism**

This philosophy says that there are many ways to God or, for that matter, there are many worldviews that are equally true that may not include God. It sounds so nice and so American, but it is not true. Jesus said, "I am the way, the truth and the life; no man comes to the Father but by Me" (John 14:6). Americans believe that all people have an equal right to believe what they want. However, as a Christian that does not mean we believe all beliefs are equally right. As an American and as a Christian, I defend your right to be wrong, but I also defend my right and responsibility before God to tell you that you are wrong according to the Scripture. This is to be done in love, humility, patience, and compassion but it needs to be done (2 Tim. 2:23-26).

**Materialism**

This philosophy lives for things that are material and measurable. If all there is to this life is the material things, then get all you can and live as long as you can. The bumper sticker that proclaims, "Whoever dies with the most toys wins" says it all about this mindset. There is a whole segment of the church that is driven by the wealth and health gospel. They believe the Lord promises all Christians prosperity and healing today if they just can muster up enough faith. I actually heard one televangelist say that the reason he drives a Mercedes is because he has Mercedes faith. The reason the rest of us faithless knuckleheads drive Volkswagens is because we only have Volkswagen faith. These folks may be sincere, but they are sincerely wrong and are lending credence to the philosophy of materialism.

Finally, the last "ism" we will mention is:

## Pragmatism

The first question that the pragmatic person asks is "Will this work?" Rarely is it important to the pragmatic person whether or not something is true. Every issue is looked at through the lens of their agenda. As long as something will profit their plans, they do not concern themselves with its veracity. Pragmatism is the order of the day for most politicians in America. Right or wrong becomes secondary; votes rule the day. In churches, church members have the vote—they vote with their wallet or their feet.

Churches that operate according to this philosophy usually have the "end justifies the means" attitude. I have been in discussions with pastors over the years about some fairly important doctrinal errors that we agreed existed in the teachings of pastors of some large churches. To my amazement, when I pointed out these errors, the supporters of these men did not defend their position biblically but simply cited the success and size of these ministries. This is a dangerous road to go down and, given enough time, will undermine the church's respect for God's Word. Success at any price is conforming to this world's system.

## The Transforming Tool of the Word of God

We have reviewed some of the temptations to conform our minds to this world's way of thinking, and now we are going to examine God's tool to transform our mind. This tool is the Word of God. Martin Luther said of the Bible, "The Bible is alive, it speaks to me; it has feet, it runs after me; it has hands, it lays hold of me. My conscience has been taken captive by the Word of God, and to go against conscience or Scripture is neither right nor safe."

Hosea 4:6 warns us that "My people are destroyed for lack of knowledge." Many churches are dead and dying due to the lack of knowledge of God's Word. There is a movement among churches to replace Bible study with fellowship alone. Now, I love fellowship, and God wants us to have fellowship, but it should not come at the expense of growing in the knowledge of the Word. While I am sure that fellowship might keep someone in church, it is the Word of God that places someone in Christ (1 Pet. 1:23). I am also sure that people love to sit around and give their opinions about particular passages, but I would much prefer to hear God's gift to the church, a pastor/teacher, edify God's people after he has prayerfully prepared (Eph. 4:11-12). Perhaps he could take questions about his lesson, but he must teach the Word.

The Bible warns that great caution is to be taken before someone puts on the mantel of a teacher of God's Word (James 3:1). I enjoy hearing people's opinion about things like sports, politics, and investments. But the Bible is God's Holy Word, and it is not meant to be placed in the blender of public opinion, swirled around, and then dished out willy-nilly. Some Bible study discussions to which I have been privy were borderline in terms of dishonoring to God's Word. I am sure this may offend some, but I believe I am on solid biblical ground when I plead with churches to be very careful about this subject. Sunday school or adult bible fellowship (ABF) or whatever you choose to call it, you had better have a God-anointed teacher expounding the Word of God. Come to my house for fellowship or meet me at Denny's for coffee, but at church I want to hear from God's Word!

In the Sept. 12, 1977 edition of Christianity Today, Billy Graham was asked if he had his life to do over again what he would change. His answer: "One of my greatest regrets is that I have not studied enough. I wish I had studied more and preached less. People have pressured me to speak to groups when I should have been studying and preparing. Donald Gray Barnhouse said that if he knew the Lord was returning in three years, he would spend two of them studying and one preaching. I'm trying to make it up." Acts 6 tells of the value God places on the study of His Word and on the prayer life of His church leaders.

## The Inerrancy and Sufficiency of the Scriptures

Thank God for the many churches that have faithfully believed and taught the inerrancy of Scripture. Indeed, we do believe that God's Word is completely true and without error from cover to cover.

However, the mind of the modern church is being deceived about the sufficiency of Scripture. Many no longer believe that the Bible alone is enough for the salvation of souls. We are witnessing a whole movement today that says you have to have signs and wonders for people to get saved. Now I trust that God can do marvelous wonders if He chooses to, and I am not trying to discourage anyone's faith in our Almighty God, but it is the Word of God that the Holy Spirit of God uses to bring forth children of God (1 Pet. 1:22-25).

Some believe we have to sneak up on sinners by playing to their flesh, almost as though these people will get the new birth without knowing it. My wife and I recently met a man named Thomas who was originally from Ghana in Africa and now lives in the United States. I asked him if he knew Christ as his Savior. He broke out in a huge smile and proceeded to share with us his salvation testimony. When he was nine years old, there was an elderly man in his village in Ghana who was a Christian. This man was blind. One day the blind man requested that little Thomas read the Bible out loud for him. While Thomas read the Gospel of Matthew to this man, he came to Matthew 4:4, which states, "Man shall not live by bread alone but, by every word that proceedeth out of the mouth of God."

Suddenly, Thomas became very aware of the fact that the Bible is the Word of God, that whatever it teaches is true, and that he needed to obey it. It was from this encounter with the Word of God that Thomas would soon respond to the gospel's call on his life (1 Pet. 1:22-25).

The Scriptures are sufficient for our sanctification and growth as a Christian (Romans 6). Whatever we know, or do not know, of the Scripture will help or hinder this process respectively. Some believe that psychology is needed for our growth in Christ. I am not saying that all psychology is bad. However, where psychology intersects with the Bible, psychology is at best superfluous, and where psychology is at odds with the Bible, it is unwelcome. Well-known Christian psychologist and author Larry Crabb said in the Aug. 14, 1995 edition of Christianity Today, "When a patient goes to a therapist, he's really asking the therapist to do the sanctifying work that the Spirit of God does through His Word. In the end, all counseling—intentionally or not—deals with issues of sanctification. The primary context for healing, then, should be the Christian community, not the antiseptic world of a private-practice therapist."

Some people believe that we need new, special, and ongoing revelation from God. However, God's revelation (that which God has chosen to reveal to man) is complete in the Bible, and Revelation 22:18-19 warns against adding to it or taking away from it. Inspiration is the way in which God has chosen to make His revelation known to man in written form. This is how we received the Bible. Second Timothy 3:16 tells us that all Scripture is God-breathed (inspiration) and is profitable for doctrine, for reproof, for correction, for instruction in righteousness, that the man of God may be perfect (mature) and completely equipped for all good works.

Revelation and inspiration are no longer, in the biblical sense, going on today. (It is true that God does reveal His existence and power in His creation, but not in a saving way.) When the canon of Scripture, the Bible, was complete, revelation and inspiration were complete. What we have for our growth and guidance today is illumination, the ability to spiritually understand God's revelation as inspired in the Word of God. Illumination is the work of the Holy Spirit turning the light on for us to see the truth that has always been there but was formerly unseen by us (1 Cor. 2:1-14). We do not need new revelation but regular illumination of God's truth to our hearts, even as the psalmist prayed, "Open thou mine eyes, that I may behold wondrous things out of Thy Law" (Ps. 119:18).

Some churches and Christians today insist that they have received new revelation from God. How do we discern such information dispensed by some very gracious Christian brethren (1 John 4:1)? They will often make comments like "God told me..." or worse, "God told me to tell you..." These comments become very subjective and beyond the objectivity of the Bible's plain truth. No matter what you may believe about such activities, most people must admit the great possibilities for abuse and deception (in some cases, self-deception).

I know people who have directed their lives and their ministries almost completely from visions and signs. They were gracious and well-meaning people, but I have witnessed some very sad results as a direct consequence of these beliefs. I confronted one man several times about a few issues, but he would always fall back on his visions being superior to any "old Bible knowledge" I had. I hope it is obvious how dangerous those beliefs can be, even if they do not manifest themselves in such extreme behavior. Teachings like that can produce within the church a breeding ground of deception, confusion, manipulation, emotionalism, and all manner of other mischief, not to mention gross ignorance of the Bible!

If Christians are told that they only need a vision from the Spirit, who needs a verse from the Scripture? Studying the Word of God becomes inferior and unspiritual to these modern Gnostics who are blessed with extra knowledge. At least seven times Paul and Peter express their desires for God's people not to be ignorant of various Bible truths. The apostle Paul repeatedly asked this question with astonishment to the Romans and Corinthians: "Know ye not…?" At least twelve times he utters his disappointment that these believers did not know some important doctrine that would enhance their walk with God.

Someone needs to protest loud and clear to the churches in America, "Know ye not…?" Someone needs to confront the pastors and Bible teachers of America with questions similar to the one Jesus asked Nicodemus in John 3:10: "Art thou a master (teacher, rabbi) in Israel, and knowest not these things?"

"God has condescended to become an author, and yet people will not read his writings. There are very few that ever gave this Book of God, the grand charter of salvation, one fair reading through." George Whitefield made this statement over two hundred fifty years ago. The Word of God gives substance and foundation to our faith (Rom. 10:17). The Bible stabilizes us in times of trials and tribulations (Ps. 119:107, 143). The study of the Bible is commanded because it helps us to correctly use it (2 Tim. 2:15). The study of the Bible gives us confidence in our walk with God (2 Tim. 1:12). The Word is sufficient to help us detect and confront error (Ps. 119:110; Heb. 4:12). The Bible is sufficient to filter out our fears and superstitions (Col. 2:7-8). Let this mind be in you, which was also in Christ Jesus (Phil. 2:5).

## Transforming the Mind through Psalms, Hymns, and Spiritual Songs

Martin Luther said that the hymn book is second only to the Bible in its importance to the church and the Christian. I say "amen" to that assessment. "Let the Word of Christ dwell in you richly in all wisdom; teaching and admonishing one another in psalms, and hymns, and spiritual songs, singing with grace in your hearts to the Lord" (Col. 3:16). It is clear from this text that singing songs is a crucial conduit in relaying biblical truth to God's people. Many churches want to argue about the style of music, but we do not have a style defined in the Bible. Yes, I have heard some well-meaning folks try to read into the Bible a style and I respect these dear brethren. However, I am not convinced that the Bible spells out and commands a certain style of music.

I think it is interesting that we have the words, and the truth they convey, preserved in the Psalms, but we do not have the music. It is obvious that God was concerned more about the words rather than the style of music. Those who would only use their very narrow interpretation of the style of music need to be careful of saying something God has not said. Those who are enamored of a particular style of music as opposed to another (conservative or contemporary) might have also been too busy critiquing the donkey Jesus was being carried into Jerusalem on and may have totally ignored the King of Kings. Let us be careful not to become what I have coined as 'donkey-detailers'. Our Lord may get lost and dishonored in the process.

Now I like all kinds of music, but my preference is more conservative than that of some folks. Notice I said preference. What I really concern myself with is the content of what is being sung. I was previewing a song once for our service at the church. The music was beautiful, and the young woman singing had a wonderful voice. I was blessed emotionally, but as I listened closely to the message the words conveyed, I was very disappointed. I could not allow her to sing the song in church, because it was teaching false doctrine about the Lord Jesus. About two years later I was in another church where this same song was used. To the pastor's credit I was told that he caught the same problem with the lyrics that I had and was not pleased by the song's subtle attack on the deity of Christ.

However, in many American churches the music is graded similar to the way a record was graded on the old American Bandstand show hosted by Dick Clark. "It has a good beat, and I can dance to it" was the popular response by teenagers who were asked about a new record release. I trust God will grant us better discernment. The issue is not whether it is contemporary, conservative, Southern gospel, or classical. The main focus must be on edifying God's people in God's Word and bringing praise and honor to God. It is not the volume of the music played but the veracity of the truth proclaimed that really matters.

I enjoy many of the old hymns not because they are old but because of their willingness to set forth solid Bible doctrine. Most of them are not mindless chants but thought-provoking vehicles of eternal truth. I have stood by the bedside of many senior saints in nursing homes over the years. I am always amazed how some who can no longer remember their own name can still sing along with me every word of "Amazing Grace," "How Great Thou Art," "In the Garden," "And Can It Be," "The Old Rugged Cross," or "Rock of Ages."

Music is a powerful tool that can be used to penetrate our hearts and minds with the Word of God. However, the enemy of our souls is aware of music's influence and uses it to transmit to our minds many of the "isms" previously discussed. The church and her people must be careful of false philosophies and doctrines being conveyed through popular music no matter what the style. My prayer is that God will continue to raise up some great Christian poets and song-writers for the next generation of churches.

The Bible reveals the mind of God—learn it!
The Bible reveals the heart of God—love it!
The Bible reveals the will of God—live it!

# How Firm a Foundation

How firm a foundation, ye saints of the Lord,
Is laid for your faith in His excellent Word!
What more can He say than to you He hath said.
To you who for refuge to Jesus have fled?

Fear not, I am with thee, O be not dismayed,
For I am thy God, and will still give thee aid;
I'll strengthen thee, help thee, and cause thee to stand,
Upheld by My gracious, omnipotent hand.

When thro' the deep waters I call thee to go,
The rivers of sorrow shall not overflow;
For I will be with thee thy trials to bless,
And sanctify to thee thy deepest distress.

When thro' fiery trails thy pathway shall lie,
My grace all sufficient, shall be thy supply;
The flames shall not hurt thee, I only design,
Thy dross to consume, and thy gold to refine.

—Unknown

# Hardened Hearts

Wherefore, as the Holy Ghost saith, Today if ye will hear His voice, Harden not your hearts, as in the provocation, in the day of temptation in the wilderness: Take heed, brethren, lest there be in any of you an evil heart of unbelief, in departing from the living God. While it is said, "Today if ye will hear His voice, harden not your hearts, as in the provocation."—Heb. 3:7-8, 12

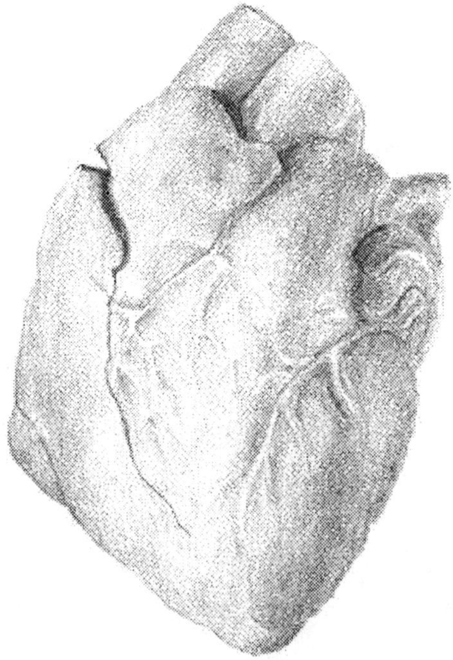

# Chapter 6

# Hardened Hearts

Our autopsy brings us to the all-important heart. The heart is the pump that distributes life-giving blood throughout the body. Heart disease, and subsequent failure, is the leading cause of death for men and women in America. Atherosclerosis, hardening of the arteries of the heart, is a common disease. Over time plaque builds up inside these arteries and blocks the flow of blood. This process has a hardening, or toughening, effect on the heart. Untreated, the disease gets worse and usually ends in heart failure. The word "sclerosis" means to harden or make tough. This word stems from the Greek word skleruno, which means hardened or stubborn, and it is that word that is the basis for the word "harden" in the Hebrews 3 text quoted previously.

The heart is the seat of our emotions, motives, and will. Out of the heart comes the true essence of what we believe (Prov. 4:23; Matt. 6:21).The heart is the source of the words with which we communicate our deepest feelings, such as fear, anger, joy, hope, faith, and love (Matt. 12:34-37). In the previous chapter we saw how the mind informs the heart by what it takes in and accepts as truth. The dead church we are now examining has had extensive heart damage due to gradual development of hardening. This has taken place over years as the people of the church repeatedly acted in unbelief toward God and His commands.

The writer to the Hebrews elaborates on the condition of such people and warns of having an "evil heart of unbelief" (Heb. 3:11). Every time a person is exposed to the truth of God's Word and chooses not to respond in obedience, that person or church is acting in unbelief. These same people are having their spiritual hearts hardened. The term "stiff-necked" is of a similar meaning and refers to an animal in a harness that refuses to be guided or directed by its owner. A person who is repeatedly refusing to obey God's Word is considered stiff-necked (Acts 7:51).

By using the ancient example of the Israelites at the time of Moses, Hebrews 3:7-15 is addressing the first-century Hebrew church. These Israelites had experienced God's power in their deliverance out of the bondage of Egypt. They saw firsthand the way God destroyed the Egyptians through the plagues. They saw God open the Red Sea to deliver them from the Egyptian army. They witnessed the feeding of the whole nation of Israel in the desert with manna from heaven and water from a rock. God even supplied them with quail for meat. Beyond all this, they were given the privilege of receiving the law of God directly from the hand of God.

Yet, even with all these blessings and wonderful evidences of God's love and care for them, the Israelites still refused to trust God. Through repeated occurrences of ingratitude and unbelief, their hearts had been hardened. Finally, because of their unbelief, the people rejected the Lord's leading into the land of promise. The Lord judged them and condemned them to wander for forty years in the wilderness.

Sadly, this is the case of some dead and dying churches in America. They are wandering around the religious and social landscape of our nation being blown to and fro by every wind of doctrine that comes along. These churches are full of people who have heard the gospel of Jesus Christ over and over and over again, but they have never really entered into a saving relationship with Christ. They have become hardened and unresponsive to God's Word. They, like many of the Hebrews, have seen God work in the lives of many others. They have many of the trappings of religion and church traditions. They have all the right words to say about church and about God, but they have never entered into Christ because of unbelief. They have the precious privilege of hearing the words inspired by the Holy Spirit (Heb. 3:7); however, the proof of a good Bible study is not a swollen head of arrogance but a stirred-up heart of action. These people have the warning about the petrifying process of the hardening of their hearts (Heb. 3:8, 13). God has given them the local church to be a positive persuasion and tells them to exhort one another daily (Heb. 3:13). God makes a personal and passionate plea for them to respond: "Today if you will hear His voice" (Heb. 3:7, 13, 15).

One of the devil's greatest wiles is convincing people that they can get saved in a little while. Satan does not care if a person decides to trust Christ tomorrow. "I will do it tomorrow" is very dangerous when God commands it today. Every day of disobedience adds to the hardness of the heart and deepens the rut of rebellion. Many in our American churches have intellectually grasped the gospel but have never had it penetrate their heart. They may have catechism, but they do not have Christ. They have the juice of the Lord's Supper, but they do not have Jesus the Lord and Savior.

In the summer of 1983, my wife and I were working with many of the Mexican immigrants who populated South Chicago. We were attending Bible college and had a church bus route that brought about seventy-five people to church every Sunday morning and evening. We would visit the area from 10 a.m. until 6 p.m. each Saturday to follow up on our riders and seek out new people with whom we could share the gospel. It was my first taste of shepherding people and was almost like pastoring a small church.

This particular June morning we met two young men who were standing outside their mother's home. We walked up to them, and Iris greeted them in Spanish, but they responded in English. I was glad because they looked like tough gang members, and I really preferred to not have to speak with them through my wife. They were brothers. Abraham was fifteen years old and Angel was sixteen. We made conversation with them for about an hour and found them to be very pleasant and open to the gospel. We asked them if they would like to repent and ask Christ to save them from their sins. They expressed an interest, but they felt they did not want to become Christians at that moment. They were not ready to leave the gang life, which was full of sin. They said they would do it later.

We saw them twice after that at their home, and again they were interested and kind, but they resisted committing their lives to Christ. "Sometime soon," they said. We were returning to the Chicago neighborhood from church services several weeks later on a hot Sunday afternoon when a young man jumped on our bus with the bad news. "Did you hear about Abraham and Angel? They were shot by rival gang members as they left a movie theater about an hour ago. Abraham was shot in the heart and died instantly. Angel was shot in the face and is in critical condition."

Iris and I were stunned. All I could think was how different it would have been if only they had given their lives to Christ a week or two earlier. They may have been in church with us instead of being shot. Angel did miraculously survive and gave his life to Christ. He eventually went off to Bible college and became a youth pastor. Abraham went out into eternity at the age of fifteen thinking he would have his whole life to get right with God. Our lives are as a vapor that appears for a little time and then vanishes. Therefore, if we know what God wants us to do and we do not do it, it is sin (James 4:13-17). While it is today, harden not your heart.

If you have never truly trusted Christ as your Savior and you want to overcome this hardened heart of unbelief, call on Him this very moment in the privacy of your own heart. The writer to the Hebrews warns: "How shall we escape if we neglect so great a salvation?" (Heb. 2:3). And Paul writes, "Behold, now is the day of salvation" (2 Cor. 6:2). Ask God to open your heart to believe, even as He opened Lydia's heart (Acts 16:14). Ask the Lord to help you overcome your unbelief (Mark 9:24). If you have such a desire, it is because the Lord is working in your life and calling you to Himself.

**Gratitude: The antidote to a hardened heart.**

Gratitude is a vital attitude in keeping the Christian's heart from being hardened with unbelief. The first sin committed in the universe was manufactured from the proud heart of Satan. He was ungrateful for all that God had given him. His beauty, his power, and his position of great influence were not enough for Satan (Ezek. 28:12-15; Isa. 14:12-15). This ingratitude was manifested in discontentment, rebellion, and disobedience. Satan then tempted Adam and Eve with the same type of ungratefulness. God had given Adam and Eve dominion over all the earth. He had provided all that they needed. God had only denied them access to one tree. Adam and Eve's ingratitude moved them to discontentment, unbelief, rebellion, and disobedience.

We previously rehearsed the same process that repeatedly surfaced in the nation of Israel. After all God had done for them, the people of Israel kept murmuring and complaining. They were ungrateful for the blessings the Lord had given them. After moaning in discontent all the way to the Promised Land, they turned back from entering the land that was filled with milk and honey. They were reduced to wandering around the desert. Yes, God did still provide for them, but they never witnessed the great victory God wanted them to have, if they had only trusted and obeyed Him.

This is the grave danger of having an ungrateful heart. The individuals will focus mainly on what they do not have and want, dwelling on their misconceived notions of how God has disappointed them. They may rarely articulate these thoughts, but these ideas infest the mind and poison it against God's goodness and faithfulness. This develops doubt, discontentment, bitterness, and a cynical attitude toward God. Faith cannot grow in this atmosphere. Quite the contrary, it is a breeding ground for unbelief, rebellion, and all types of moral impurities (Rom. 1:18-32). You show me an ungrateful person, and I will show you a hard-hearted person.

Some churches are man-centered and are geared to play up to the selfishness of the flesh. The congregation is wandering through the motions religiously. Service to service, promotion to promotion, and program to program, they slouch through. Sunday after Sunday, they become critics of sermon delivery (rarely of content, because the truth would challenge them to change)—tasting a little truth here and a little truth there, but never really ingesting and digesting the whole truth to the nourishing of their spiritual lives.

In these churches there is rarely an open, honest plea for people to act on the truth preached. The people for the most part are entertained by the worship rather than entering into the worship of the Lord. (These churches are geared toward keeping you comfortably in the pew and your tithe in the plate.) There are few real victories, because they never really join the battle. The buildings are big, the budgets are bigger, and the body count continually increases. They think themselves rich, but they are really spiritually poor. They have become lukewarm, which is the very essence of uselessness. The Lord Jesus Christ is actually left outside of this big, busy, and wealthy church, knocking at the door (see the Laodicean church of Rev. 3:14-22).

Finally, the hardened heart is given over to an evil heart of unbelief. Proverbs 29:1 warns that a person who has been often reproved and hardens their neck against God shall be destroyed suddenly, without any remedy. These are sober words and should be heeded by all of us.

**How can we cultivate a grateful heart?**

*Remember all that the Lord has done for you.* If there was one sin that the Israelite people continued to fall back into, it was murmuring and complaining against God. And if there was one command that the Lord kept repeating through His prophets to His people, it was to remember and do not forget. Take a Bible concordance sometime and look up how many times these words, and their derivatives, are used about the Israelites. Time and time again they would forget God's goodness to them. And when they forgot, they always rebelled and their morals rapidly declined. God gave them the Passover meal to help them remember how He delivered them from bondage. Every Sabbath day was to be a remembrance to the Jewish people of what the Lord had done for them.

The church has been given the Lord's Supper to regularly remember what Jesus Christ has done for us on the cross. The church that is alive is a church that regularly observes the Lord's Supper in a reverent and meaningful way. This observance should not be just ceremonial but a soul-searching experience for the congregation. Gratitude for the sacrificial death of Christ should be humbly acknowledged.

I am typing these words on November 11, Veterans Day. I just watched a program dedicated to the men and women who served our country during World War II. Every time I see something like that, my heart swells with gratitude for these brave people. I live only minutes from Bedford, Virginia, where the D-Day Memorial regularly reminds us of what others have sacrificed for our freedom. How much more does the memorial of the Lord's Supper warm my heart towards the Savior, who gave His all for me! Whenever I sense my heart getting cold and hard, I simply stop and think about the bondage from which the Lord has saved me. I thank Him for how He has blessed me beyond anything I could have imagined. I immerse myself in His grace, and I am humbled to tears. It is amazing how much more loving and patient I then become of others. Suddenly, the weakness of others pales in comparison to what I know God has forgiven in me. When I consider my sins, which are many, being forgiven by Him, I am able to love much more and obey His commands more readily (Luke 7:41-47).

*Rejoice in corporate songs of praise for what the Lord has done for you.* Remembering God's blessings during corporate singing of praise and worship is vital to keeping the heart of the church tender toward God. Songs that have been breathed upon by the Holy Spirit and sung by lips that are devoted to Christ are a powerful force. God created the universe within an atmosphere of singing (Job 38:4-7). Song is the source of joy, hope, and deliverance when our souls are in a dark night of discouragement (Job 35:10; Ps. 32:6-7). Singing is an instrument available to us to help conquer the enemies of our faith (2 Chron. 20:21-22). and it conveys Bible truth to our hearts (Col. 3:16). A good worship leader, not just a song leader, is vital to the church services, for they can weave Scripture, songs, and comments into an edifying service of praise and thanksgiving.

*Remember what others have done for you.* Having an attitude of gratitude towards others is essential to keeping our hearts right not only with God but also with others. The apostle Paul in his letters gives thanks no less than ten times for the fellow believers he knew and loved. He was not afraid to express this gratitude, and we should not be either. Because of our fallen nature, we are much more ready to see the negative aspects of our friends and acquaintances rather than the way they have blessed our lives. The church should be a place where God's people are encouraged to express their love and thankfulness to one another. This atmosphere nurtures a love for God, because it is His love that has brought us together. It is because

God has initiated and poured out His love on us that we can express love to one another (Rom. 5:5).

Recently I was at a gathering of many of the people from the church I started in Pennsylvania. I watched as the folks greeted each other in Christian love. They laughed and genuinely enjoyed each other's fellowship. They were thankful for each other. I was thankful for how many of them were a blessing to me and my family. As I drove away, I mentioned to my wife how it was because of Jesus that most of us knew each other. This thought made me love Christ more.

*Realize what God has planned for you.* The Lord has promised to conform you to the image of His Son, Jesus Christ, and that all things will work together for your good (Rom. 8:29-29). He will never leave you or forsake you (Heb. 13:5-6). Jesus has gone to heaven to prepare a place for you, and He promises to return to take you there to dwell with Him (John 14:1-6). Revelation 21 and 22 tell of the glorious heavenly home the Lord has prepared for you and me as believers. He will wipe away every tear from our eyes. No more death, no more pain, and no more sorrow will ever be allowed in heaven. Every time I read these passages my heart is moved with affection for the Lord, and I want to love and serve Him better. The church that is alive believes in a literal heaven and preaches about it.

I trust you and your church will examine your hearts to see if it is in the process of hardening. Has God been speaking to you about something in your life? Has the Lord told you to stop doing something you know displeases Him? Perhaps the Lord has directed you to start doing something you have refused to do. Today is the day to start obeying! Have you been taking the Lord's goodness for granted? Let the goodness of the Lord lead you to repentance (Rom. 2:4).

# Since Jesus Came into My Heart

What a wonderful change in my life has been wrought
Since Jesus came into my heart!
I have light in my soul for which long I had sought,
Since Jesus came into my heart!

I have ceased from my wandering and going astray
Since Jesus came into my heart!
And my sins, which were many, are all washed away,
Since Jesus came into my heart!

I shall go there to dwell in that city, I know,
Since Jesus came into my heart!
And I'm happy, as onward I go,
Since Jesus came into my heart!

—Rufus H. McDaniel

# Itching Ears

For the time will come when they will not endure sound doctrine; but after their own lust shall they heap to themselves teachers, having itching ears; And they shall turn away theirs ears from the truth, and shall be turned unto fables.—2 Tim. 4:3-4

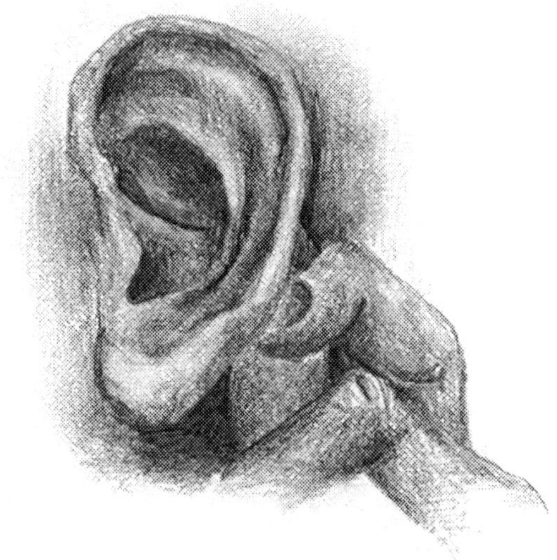

## Chapter 7

# Itching Ears

There are allergies and infections that can cause this itching of the ears. If left untreated, an infection could damage the ear drums. This would certainly not be a cause of death but could cause loss of hearing. We have before us a dead church that has ear damage. There seem to be scratching marks on the inside of the ears. The cause of this itching is the desire of the church people to hear what they want to hear and not what they need to hear. This is a sure way for the church to become very ill and even die.

In 2 Timothy 4:2-4, the apostle Paul admonishes Timothy to be ready to preach the Word at all times. Timothy was to reprove, rebuke, and exhort with patience, because there would not always be the positive results he desired. The preacher must preach Bible doctrine and not his opinion, manmade philosophy, psychology, sociology, or religious speeches. There will be a temptation not to preach the Bible in the last days, because people will want to turn away from the truth and will prefer fables that make them feel good about their lives of sin. They will seek out teachers who will fulfill their craving for lies that rebel against God's truth.

### The Temptation to Tickle Ears

All you need to do is look at some of the most popular speakers (I hesitate to dignify them with the term "preachers") today, and you will find them telling people what they want to hear. They never call sin what it is—sin. It is usually referred to as a mistake. They seek to rename wicked behavior so as to take away its stigma and guilt. These false teachers find an open market for their teachings because people have real guilt and are looking for relief. The people find false refuge in these unscriptural teachings.

There is a false sense of security, because all of this manmade philosophy is disguised as being dispensed by men of God. However, one day God will sweep away this refuge of lies and judge people by the truth (Isa. 28:17). In 2 Chronicles 18, we find an ill-advised alliance of the southern kingdom of Judah and her good King Jehoshaphat with the northern kingdom of Israel and her evil King Ahab. This was one of the most unequally yoked pair of leaders in history. They certainly had nothing in common spiritually, but Ahab wanted Jehoshaphat's help in making war with Syria.

These two kings were trying to decide whether they should go up to battle with their combined forces to the city of Ramoth-gilead. Jehoshaphat asked Ahab to call together some prophets and inquire of the Lord, through them, as to whether they should make this attack. Instead, Ahab had four hundred of his prophets tell him what he wanted to hear: go up to battle, and you will win. Jehoshaphat had enough discernment to realize these were prophets of Baal (a false god) and that he wanted to hear from God's prophet. He asked Ahab if there was a prophet of the Lord at hand of whom to inquire what they should do.

Ahab reluctantly tells Jehoshaphat that there is a prophet of the Lord called Micaiah, but that this prophet never tells Ahab what he wants to hear; thus, Ahab hates him. However, at the insistence of Jehoshaphat, Ahab sends for the prophet Micaiah. Even the servant who is sent to get Micaiah tries to persuade the prophet to go along with the crowd of four hundred false prophets and tell Ahab what he wanted to hear. After Micaiah came before the kings, he sarcastically tells Ahab to go up to the battle. Ahab gets angry because he knows that Micaiah is mocking him. Micaiah gets serious and tells Ahab that the Lord will allow the kings to go up to battle, but they will lose the battle and Ahab will be killed. Ahab was furious and had Micaiah thrown in prison. The kings did go up to battle and were defeated. Ahab was killed, and the people were scattered just as Micaiah had prophesied. Ahab had his itching ears tickled, but it cost him his life.

Everyone likes to be liked. No preacher who is mentally and emotionally healthy wants people to dislike him. But the preacher must tell the people what God wants them to hear and not what the people want to hear. God never tells us to take a survey so that the people in the pew can decide what they will hear from the pulpit. (He never tells us to take a survey to decide what kind of church to build, either.) No governing board of deacons or elders has a right to threaten a preacher to curb God's message (notice I did not say "the preacher's message").

As a pastor of a church, one reason I preached expositional messages through books of the Bible was that it forced me to give the whole counsel of God no matter how hard it would hit me or anyone else. Whatever the next verse said was what I preached. It did not matter whose foot it might step on. Proverbs 29:25 says that the fear of man will bring you into a snare (trap). The pastor of a church should not be manipulated into being a pleaser of men. When man is big in our sight, God becomes small. We must see God as bigger than any man and fear only God (Heb. 13:6).

The tickling of people's ears is a great temptation for any pastor. Not only does he get subtle pressure from his congregation, but also there is peer pressure from his fellow pastors or denomination. There are always those who will cut you off from fellowship if you do not agree with them on all their issues. People are always trying to push you into their little mold or denomination. For over twenty years I have not sought to take on any denomination's name or creed. The two churches I have helped to plant did not have a denomination's name. I am not against someone else who is comfortable with these names or denominations, but I have just not chosen to join the club. I know without a doubt that if I had kept my mouth shut and gone along with the program, I could have advanced and built some earthly security within a particular group. But I have seen some things going on in some of these churches that are not scriptural, and I have spoken out about them rather than just going along to get along.

There are men in pulpits all over America who are fearful of standing up for what they know the Bible teaches just so they can keep their comfortable positions. I have spoken with some privately. Some men whose denominations have gone down the road to gross error are fearful to speak out. I was visiting a pastor in his study years ago on Staten Island. He told me that he would love to have the freedom to preach what he believed the Bible taught, but if he did, he would have to resign his pulpit and leave his denomination.

My heart hurts for men who are in bondage of pleasing other men so they can keep their prestige, position, and pensions. The politics of the pulpit is infecting our churches and causing men to tickle ears that are itching to hear anything but God's convicting truth. No preacher is above this temptation. Even the apostle Peter gave in to the legalistic Judaizers and had to be rebuked by the apostle Paul in Galatians 2:11-12. Peter's fear of man caused him to change his message. Peter's fear of man actually caused him to deny the Lord (Luke 22:54-62). I want people to like me, and I am not by nature a confrontational person, but I simply cannot set aside what I believe the Bible says about a matter just so people will not think ill of me. I am not advocating being unkind but simply speaking the truth in love (Eph. 4:15).

Think about these very frank and bold words Jesus said to the Pharisees in His day: "I am come in My Father's name, and ye receive me not: if another shall come in his own name, him ye will receive. How can ye believe, which receive honor one of another, and seek not honor that comes from God only?" (John 5:43-44). The Lord bluntly says that if we are looking for the honor of other people then you are not going to be open to God's truth. When we live in fear of man, we stifle our understanding of God's Word because we must always read it through the filter of the group or person we seek to impress.

An interesting experience that I have had is that many of the very hard-edged fundamentalists believe they are the only ones bold enough to speak up for truth. The fact of the matter is there are some in that circle who are so browbeaten by their peers they are afraid to have any opinion that does not square with the teachings of whatever evangelical or Baptist "pope" they are beholden to. They are deathly afraid of hearing that "L" word—liberal (and I do not mean a Democrat). And you will here it loud and clear if you miss a "ye," "thee," or "thou" in your Bible quotations. Also, if you even mention the Bible word "election" you will be slapped with the "C" word – Calvinist.

When I am with some charismatic Christians, they expect me to be open-minded to their way of thinking and dismiss me as a lesser grade of Christian because I disagree with them on some issues concerning the gifts of the Spirit. I am one of the poor "U"—unfilled. And there are some of my reformed friends who are always judging to see if you are reformed enough. To them, anything less than a five-point Calvinist makes your salvation testimony suspect, and you could be called the "A" word—Arminian. Then there are some of the more progressive Bible evangelicals who cannot help calling anyone with some modest and appropriate standards the dreaded "P" word—Pharisee!

We love labels. They keep everyone nicely and neatly in their place. I have friends in all these camps, and many others, whom I love dearly and respect immensely, but I will not let that deter me from what I believe the Bible teaches about any subject. I will not seek to tickle their ears, nor do I require them to tickle mine. Quite the contrary, I admire another believer who will tell you the truth about what they believe according to the Scripture and allow you to respectfully disagree.

Consider and reflect on these passages:

In God I will praise His Word, in God I have put my trust; I will not fear what flesh can do unto me.—Ps. 56:4

The Lord is on my side; I will not fear: What can man do unto me?—Ps. 118:6

It is better to trust in the Lord than to put confidence in man. It is better to trust in the Lord than to put confidence in princes.—Ps. 118:8-9

Cursed is the man that trusteth in man, and maketh flesh his arm, and whose heart departeth from the Lord.—Jer. 17:5

Nevertheless among the chief rulers also many believed on Him; but because of the Pharisees did not confess Him, lest they should be put out of the synagogue: For they loved the praise of men more than the praise of God.—John 12:42-43

For do I now persuade men, or God? Or do I please men? For if I yet please men, I should not be the servant of Christ.—Gal.1:10

So that we may boldly say, The Lord is my helper, and I will not fear what man shall do unto me.—Heb. 13:6

We have thus far been challenging the ear ticklers (preachers) not to give in to the temptation as man-pleasers but to preach the Word. We are now going to turn our attention to the itching ears. How can we get the most out of a Bible sermon?

**Take Heed How You Hear!**

It takes good listening as well as good preaching to make a good sermon. Jesus was the greatest preacher there ever was, and the sermon of the sower, the seed, and the soils is one of the greatest sermons ever preached (Matt. 13:1-9; 18-23; Mark 4:1-29; Luke 8:4-15). In this sermon Jesus tells of how the kingdom of God is like a sower (Jesus Christ and His servants sharing the Word of God) going out to scatter the seed (the Word of God) onto different types of soil (hearts of men). The emphasis is on the hearer (soil) of the Word (the word "hear" is used nine times in this section). The sower is the same, and the seed is the same, but the soil is the variable (the inconsistent ingredient).

I believe the contextual understanding of these passages has to do with the response of people to the gospel. However, I think there is a very valid application of a Christian's response to the teaching of God's Word. This will be the content of the remainder of this chapter. Soil preparation and cultivation is vital to the growth of any seed planted. So it is with the planting of God's Word (the seed) in our heart (soil). The parable of the soils is mentioned three times in the gospels, and Jesus ends each one with a slightly different twist of a familiar exhortation. In Matthew 13:9, He says, "Who has ears to hear let him hear!" In Mark 4:24, it's "Take heed what you hear!" And in Luke 8:18, He says, "Take heed how you hear!" We must hear God's Word so that we can grow in faith (Rom. 10:17). What we hear must be the Word of God and not the fables and stories of men. However, how we hear will make the difference in the fruit that will be produced.

**Soil Preparation and Cultivation**

*Before the sermon, prepare your heart with these considerations*:

Consider the fact that hearing is not enough. The prophet Ezekiel had a reputation for being a very eloquent and dynamic preacher. The people said he was like a lovely singer who can play an instrument well. However, these same people did not listen with the intent to obey God's warnings or commands. With their mouth they showed much love, but with their hearts they pursued their own gain (Ezek. 33:30-33). These people were like many Christian "conference junkies" in America today. They go from conference to conference hearing all the biggest and the best speakers. They even take volumes of notes, but they put very little into practice. In fact, they might break your leg or verbally assault you if you were to slide their Bible over and sit in their choice seat at the conference.

Sound familiar? The writer of Hebrews mentions those who heard the Word of God, but it did not profit them because they did not mix their hearing with faith (Heb. 4:1-2). James warns us not to be self-deceived by being only hearers of the Word and not doers also (James 1:22-25).

Consider the fact that we are hearing God's Word. We need to remember that as long as the preacher is rightly teaching from the Bible, it is the Word of God that we are hearing. The Thessalonians were commended by Paul for just such an attitude, and the Word of God had much fruit within that church (1 Thess. 2:13). We should have a humble reverence for God's authoritative Word, as Isaiah proclaims (Isa. 66:5). We need to hear God's Word as His very voice and respond in submission, as young Samuel did when he said, "Speak, Lord, for Your servant hears" (1 Sam. 3:9). "My sheep hear My voice, and I know them, and they follow Me," Jesus said in John 10:27.

Consider the fact that we need the Spirit's illumination to help us understand the Word. The psalmist pleads for the Lord to open his eyes to behold wonderful things out of God's Law (Ps. 119:18). What a great prayer to pray before a church service. You will be surprised at how much better the preacher will become. Solomon, in the book of Proverbs, says we should cry out to the Lord for discernment in His Word (Prov. 2:3-11). Paul tells the Corinthians that only the Spirit can teach us spiritual truth (1 Cor. 2:6-16).

Consider the fact that we need to lay aside our known sin in order to fully appreciate God's Word. Peter says that our appetite for the Word of God should be as a newborn baby's desire for his mother's milk. But, if we let sins build up in our heart we will diminish that hunger for the Bible (1 Pet. 2:1-2). James warns of the same laying aside of sin in order to receive the Word of God effectively (James 1:21).

*During the Sermon:*

Be sure to have a teachable mind. The Berean believers, as described in Acts 17:11, had a readiness of mind to learn. Some people come to church, and they know it all. No one can edify them because they have heard it all. Others come to church and are eager to learn from the Word what God has to say. I have had some dear older saints sit under my pastorate. They have heard many great preachers over the years, in person and on the radio. One woman I know has sat under the preaching of Harry Ironside, Donald G. Barnhouse, Oliver B. Green, and many more. However, this same dear woman will glean something from the least experienced preacher, as long as he uses the Bible correctly. She will let that preacher know how she was blessed and what the truth was that blessed her. She has a ready, humble, and teachable mind.

In stark contrast to the woman above, I have been around some younger preachers who know everything. Mention some truth from Scripture or some aspect of the ministry, and they will tell you all about it. I once rode along in a car with a young man who had just been ordained to the ministry. He was at least fifteen years my junior in the work of the Lord. We traveled for six hours together, and never once did he ask me a question. Now, I am no genius (I am sure you picked up on that by now), but I am sure there is something I know that he does not know. He had no readiness of mind to learn.

Be sure not to be distracted or to daydream during the sermon. Romans 7 tells of our flesh warring against our spirit. This is so evident when we start to attempt to do something spiritual like study our Bible, listen to a sermon, or pray. It seems we can so easily get drowsy or distracted while doing the most spiritual of tasks. Jesus said, "Let these sayings sink down [deeply] into your ears" (Luke 9:44). The picture here is of a people giving earnest, sincere thought to what is being said. Thinking can be hard work. It would help many of us if we did not to keep late Saturday nights. Too often people come dragging into church barely awake and unfit to absorb the Word of God in an effective manner. When God is communicating His Word through His servant, He uses every part of that man—his body language, facial expression, voice inflection, and so forth—and I want to take all that in so as to get all that God has for me. If my mind is not fully engaged I might miss some truth God has for me. Be determined to fix your mind on the nourishing of your soul.

Be sure to give a wholehearted response to the Word of God. As we have a previously considered in Hebrews 3, we do not want to have a hard heart of unbelief. Therefore, be ready to give your full response to what the Word of God says, even as you are hearing the words. A nod of the head or an "amen" or the writing down of a note about how you will apply the truth just spoken is helpful (Neh. 8:5-6, 8-9). There is an appropriate time and way for the preacher to give an invitation as the Lord moves him in the service. This gives the people of God an immediate opportunity to respond to the message of God. This is where God's Word is so different from other teachings and philosophies. It demands a verdict and a response.

Open my ears, that I may hear
Voices of truth Thou sendest clear;
And while wave notes fall on my ear,
Everything false will disappear.
Silently now wait for Thee,
Ready, my God, Thy will to see;
Open my ears, illumine me, Spirit divine.

—Clara H. Scott

*After the Sermon:*

Examination of the Scripture (Acts 17:11). After the sermon, look up cross-references and compare scriptures. While pastoring, I never became upset with a person who honestly used their Bible to get a clarification on something I taught. I was blessed to be the pastor of such diligent individuals. As the days in our country become darker, fewer people will want to know the truth. There are those who only seek to start a controversy or to postulate foolish questions to try and entrap the preacher. Most people, however, have sincere questions to which the pastor must give the answer from the Bible.

Meditation on the Scriptures given during a sermon. While the preacher is preaching, I will have my attention gripped by a verse that the pastor quotes. At the moment I cannot wander from the sermon to meditate on the text. I will jot down the reference and revisit it after the sermon. Sometimes I have stayed in the pew after the service and followed up on the verse and dwelt on its meaning. Other times I meditate on it and study it all week (Ps. 1:2; 119:15, 23, 48, 97, 148).

Application of main truths to your life. Think about what God wants you to do about the truth you have heard. Write it down. Design a plan to implement the truth. Give yourself a timetable to get started. And just do it!

Reflection on truth you have learned. Hebrews 2:1 tells us to give earnest heed to the truths we have heard lest we let them slip. The apostle Peter says he will not neglect to stir up people to remember the truth they have already received (2 Pet. 1:12-14). As I hear new sermons, I often am reminded of how they fit together with what I have learned previously from God's Word. I fondly reflect on these foundational truths, and my faith is deepened. My respect for God's Word is enhanced as I see, once again, how all of God's truth fits together. Now that is music to my ears!

# Jesus Is Calling

Jesus is tenderly calling thee home
Calling today, calling today;
Why from the sunshine of love wilt thou roam,
Farther and farther away?

Jesus is calling the weary to rest
Calling today, calling today;
Bring Him thy burden and thou shalt be blest:
He will not turn thee away.

Jesus is waiting; O, come to Him now
Waiting today, waiting today;
Come with thy sins; at His feet lowly bow;
Come, and no longer delay.

Jesus is pleading; O list to His voice:
Hear Him today, O, hear Him today;
They who believe on His name shall rejoice;
Quickly arise and away.

Calling today; calling today;
Jesus is calling, is tenderly calling today!

—Fanny Crosby

# Dry Eyes with Blurry Vision

Jesus wept.—John 11:35

Therefore watch, and remember, that by the space of three years I ceased not to warn every one night and day with tears.—Acts 20:31

Where there is no vision, the people perish.
—Prov. 29:18

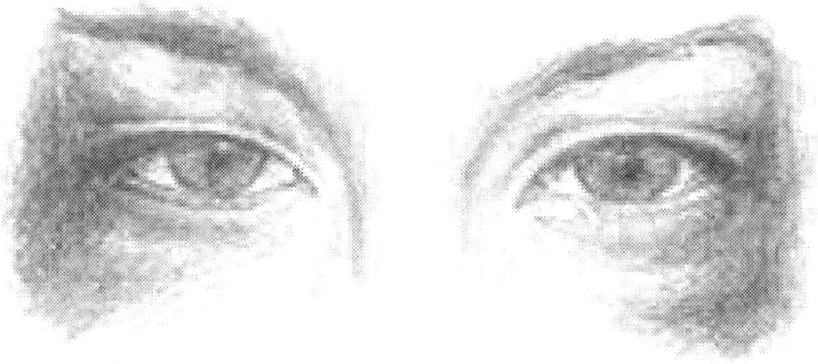

# Chapter 8

# Dry Eyes with Blurry Vision

The eyeball is kept moist and healthy by a thin film of tears that is continuously produced by the lachrymal gland situated underneath the top eyelid. Every time we blink, tears are swept toward the inside corner of eye and drained through two tiny tubes called lachrymal ducts. From there, tears pass into the nasolachrymal sac, then into the nasolachrymal duct to the nose and, ultimately, to the throat for swallowing. A blockage along any point of this tear-duct system is known as a blocked tear duct, or dacryostenosis. Without moisture, our corneas, which serve as protective domes for the front of the eyes, would dry out and become injured.

**They have lost their first love for the Lord.**

The autopsy of this dead church before us uncovers the tragedy of blocked tear ducts. This church has long ago become apathetic and indifferent to the needs of those hurting around them. They are part of the stiff upper lip and dry-eyed religious gang. Oh, if you quiz them on doctrine and church order you may find them to be very orthodox. They are, in most cases, a well-organized and well-oiled machine. They would never be called mindless Christians. They are often very intelligent Bible students. They can quote for you chapter and verse, but there is the absence of honest tears flowing from a passion for Christ and a compassion for the lost. They are working diligently, but they have lost a first love for the Lord and a true burden for people. Their theme song might well be "I Shall Not Be Moved." At this point this chapter is closely related to the hardened-heart chapter. The seat of emotions has been hardened by apathy.

The church at Ephesus is depicted in Revelation 2:1-7 as such a church. The Christians were doctrinally sound and actively serving, but there was a sense of emotional detachment from their relationship with the Lord and His work. Their service had become dry and routine. Their passion had dwindled and needed to be revived. This is the status of many dying and dead churches. This is the condition of all Christians at some time during their life in Christ.

There is a need to have the fires of desire rekindled. Any married couple can relate to the need to keep the fires of their love stoked by recommitting themselves not only to the routine of married life but also to deliberately scheduling time to maintain intimacy and emotional connection. No wife who loves her husband wants to be loved by rote but much prefers a relationship by romance. There is a vast difference! Does your church have a romance with her Redeemer or a rote relationship?

**Mary of Bethany and Her Radical Expression of Love**

Mark 14:3-9 tells a story that vividly portrays the first love of Mary of Bethany (John 12 tells us that Mary is the woman who anointed Jesus, and Judas is the one who begins the complaints against her). The twelve disciples are with Jesus in Bethany enjoying a meal with Lazarus and his sisters, Mary and Martha, about one week before our Lord's crucifixion.

Mary is suddenly moved with great love and adoration for her Lord. She pulls out an expensive alabaster box full of rare spikenard ointment. She breaks the box (it was sealed, so to gain access to the ointment the box had to be destroyed). Mary pours the ointment on Jesus as an extravagant and radical expression of her love. Everyone is stunned! This was irrational! The cost of this outpouring in today's terms would be between twenty thousand and forty thousand dollars. It is not logical or practical! This money could be used for the poor, Judas reminds everyone. The other disciples chime in with Judas. But Jesus says it is a beautiful thing that she has done. The KJV simply translates the words "good thing," but the words are better understood as "beautiful thing." It was beyond a moral duty. It was beyond reason. Math genius and theologian Blaise Pascal said hundreds of years ago, "Love has reasons that reason cannot know." Mary's heart was responding in a beautiful way that reason could not contain or comprehend.

The Holy Spirit has sandwiched this amazing story between the hatred for Jesus in Mark 14:1-2, where we find the wicked chief priest and scribes seeking to kill Jesus, and Mark 14:10, where we find Judas seeking to betray Jesus. What about the other disciples? It seems they have become somewhat indifferent to Jesus. Maybe they have become apathetic. They still wanted to do service for Him by helping the poor, but Jesus mildly rebukes them for their complacency. It is as though the Lord wants to create a black velvet backdrop on which to display the pearl of Mary's outpouring of sacrifice and love. Sometimes it takes only one Mary in a church to shake us out of our apathy by her example. It takes only one person to hear the voice of Jesus outside the church knocking on the door requesting to be given entrance into His church. Who will open the door to the Lord and let Him become the main focus again (Rev. 3:20)? It will most often take a radical expression to arrest the attention of an apathetic church!

Jesus goes on to say that wherever the gospel is preached this woman's deed would be noted. Why? I believe Jesus is implying that this radical expression of love is just the response we should all have toward the most radical expression of love ever demonstrated: Calvary! What Jesus did on the cross for you and me was not reasonable or rational. The fact that a holy God should become man and die for our unholy, undeserving race is truly an irrational, radical expression of love!

Where the whole realm of nature mine,
That were a present far too small:
Love so amazing, so divine,
Demands my soul, my life, my all.

—Isaac Watts

When was the last time you did something as a radical expression of love for Christ? How about your church? Are you just moving along in calculated, measured, duty-bound service for God? Is the tithe your standard of spiritual sacrifice? When Jesus wanted to show an example of giving, whom did He point out? Jesus directs our attention to a little widow who gave just two mites, or about four cents in contemporary terms. However, it was all she had. How rational or reasonable is that? She did not give out of her abundance but out of her poverty (Mark 12:41-44). She did not give out of her duty but out of her love. Jesus said she gave more than all of them, in His eyes.

What of the woman in Luke 7:36-50? She crashes a party that some Pharisee was throwing in honor of Jesus. She was a noted sinner who was touched by the compassion of our Lord. She stands behind Him weeping. She crumbles at His feet, kissing them, and begins to rinse them with her tears and wipe them with her hair. She, like Mary, anoints his feet with ointment. Jesus knows exactly what the Pharisees are thinking: "How undignified and unseemly is this scene? How inappropriate for her to even be here, let alone being allowed to touch Him. There is no need for this expression of public emotionalism." Jesus answers these judgmental thoughts with a parable about forgiveness, teaching that whoever really senses their great need for great forgiveness will respond with a great outpouring of love.

How would your church respond to such a person? Would the church's pharisees shake their heads and criticize the pastor for allowing too much emotionalism? Brethren, our churches need to see some honest tears flowing from all of us. We need tears of repentance as we turn from our sins. We need tears of joy when we get right with God and others get right with God. We need tears for the lost around us and around the world. We need tears of compassion for those hurting among us. People who have compassion like that can turn the world right-side up (Acts 17:6).

## If We Are the Body

It's crowded in worship today
As she slips in trying to fade into the faces
The girls teasing laughter is carrying farther than they know

Farther than they know

But if we are the body
Why aren't His arms reaching?
Why aren't His hands healing?
Why aren't His words teaching?
And if we are the body
Why aren't His feet going?
Why is His love not showing them there is a way?

There is a way

A traveler is far away from home
He sheds his coat and quietly sinks into the back row
The weight of their judgmental glances
Tells him that his chances are better out on the road

But if we are the body
Why aren't His arms reaching?
Why aren't His hands healing?
Why aren't His words teaching?
And if we are the body
Why aren't His feet going?
Why is His love not showing them there is a way?
There is a way

Jesus paid much too high a price
For us to pick and choose who should come
And we are the body of Christ

But if we are the body
Why aren't His arms reaching?
Why aren't His hands healing?
Why aren't His words teaching?
And if we are the body
Why aren't His feet going?
Why is His love not showing them there is a way?
There is a way

Jesus is the way

—Mark Hall of Casting Crowns



**The Tears of Jesus**

Jesus was no stranger to tears. Isaiah 53:3 says that He was a man of sorrows and acquainted with grief, His own grief and that of those who were around Him. Let us briefly examine some of the occasions that Jesus shed tears.

*Jesus wept tears of sympathy over the rebellion of sinners.* Jesus wept over the city of Jerusalem as He approached it a week before the people in that city would crucify Him (Luke 19:41-42). They were blinded to His true identity and would not come to Him. As the church is seeking to reach the lost, may we have a burden for those who would seemingly be the hardest and most rebellious. We are not at liberty to just write off any people or person as unreachable.

I have heard Dr. James M. Boice relate this story about an evangelist. A preacher was preaching a series of sermons in a particular town. A young woman was invited by a friend who was concerned for her soul. This visiting young lady had come to America from another country and settled in New York City. She soon got involved with the wrong crowd and was used and abused by one man after another. She became very calloused, skeptical, and distrustful. In short, she was emotionally broken.

She was unmoved by the evangelistic service. Afterwards, her friend briefly told her story to the preacher and asked that he come to the rear of the building to speak directly to this hardened young woman. He did so but found her cold and rude. He stopped, looked in her eyes, and simply asked her if he could pray for her before he let her go on her way. She at least allowed him this courtesy. He began praying for her, and immediately his heart was broken for this woman. He began to weep for her. He stopped praying and told her he could not continue. He dismissed her to leave, but she would not go. "No man has ever wept for me. You can preach to me now," she said, sobbing. Her heart was softened by the Lord with the tears of a preacher who cared enough to weep.

Is your church watering the fields surrounding it with tears of compassion? Jesus did. The apostle Paul did. The Bible says when Jesus saw the people of Jerusalem, He had compassion on them. When Paul saw the people of Athens given over to idolatry, he was moved with compassion for them (Acts 17:16). Getting outside the walls of our church to see the hurt of people will get our hearts moved with compassion. Jeremiah said that his eyes had affected his heart (Lam. 3:51). Get out to the streets of the city and see the people. Go to the mission field of Africa, India, South America, or Asia and see the people. Look in their eyes and let God break your heart for the hurting of this world.

People do not care how much you know until they know how much you care. The lost people living around our churches do not want to become a number in our church program or a notch on our award belt. They are not interested in making your church the biggest and best in the city where you live. They are not placed along our path so our children can win an Awana badge. They want someone who cares as Jesus does. Many people feel the way King David did when he lamented, "I looked on my right hand, and beheld, but there was no man that would know me; no man cared for my soul" (Ps. 142:4).

*Jesus wept tears of compassion for the results of sin.* Jesus got to the gravesite of His friend Lazarus, and He wept with those who were weeping (John 11:35). This world is experiencing the results of the sin of Adam and the sins of Adam's race. Trillions of hot, salty tears have coursed down the face of mankind since that fateful day when sin entered the world. Death, disease, pain, and sorrow are all results of this sin-cursed world. Jesus is the unseen mourner at every grave and the comforter at countless bedsides, from age to age and country to country. His church must be willing to have tears of compassion for the hurting. We do not always have the right words to say, and sometimes it would be better for us to have nothing to say. However, we can say volumes with our comforting presence and tears. Paul wrote to the Corinthians, "For out of much affliction and anguish of heart I wrote unto you with many tears; not that ye should be grieved, but that ye might know the love which I have more abundantly unto you" (2 Cor. 2:4).

*Jesus wept tears of suffering for the redemption of sinners.* Hebrews 5:7 tells us Jesus offered prayers and supplications with strong crying and tears in the garden of Gethsemane. This was all part of the passion of Christ that eventually led to His death for our sins. Does your church have Gethsemane-type prayer meetings for the salvation of souls within your sphere of influence? These are prayer meetings that declare the attitude of Christ by crying, "Not our will, Lord, but yours." Prayer warriors who declare, "Whatever it takes, Lord, please save the lost through us."

*Jesus shall one day wipe away all tears.* The Bible tells us there is coming a day in heaven that Jesus will do away with all tears, sorrow, and death (Rev. 21:1-6). Oh, what a glorious day that will be! It will not be glorious, however, this side of heaven. In the meantime, the church and her people have the privilege to follow our Lord's example in weeping tears for the lost and with the hurting.

## This Church Has Eyes That Lack Vision

This dead church that we are examining not only had dry tear ducts but also had spiritual myopia. There was no future vision for the church to fulfill God's design for its purpose. Helen Keller once said, "Poor eyes limit your sight; poor vision limits your deeds." Vision is merely hope with a blueprint. Former Senate chaplain Peter Marshall once prayed, "Give us clear vision that we may know where to stand and what to stand for, because unless we stand for something, we shall fall for anything." Aristotle said, "The soul never thinks without a picture." The church and her people need leadership with a vision.

Years ago, I was sitting in our cabin on Coventry Lake just off the campus of the University of Connecticut in the town of Storrs, CT. I was listening to music with my roommate, Nick Giaquinto. We were both in our senior year playing football for the university, and instead of living in a dorm we lived in a little house beside a lake. Suddenly, I noticed Nick smiling for no apparent reason. I asked him what was so funny. He shrugged his shoulders and chuckled. Then he proceeded to tell me that he had just run a touchdown. I asked him to elaborate, and he told me he would often run whole plays out in his mind. He would take a hand-off, stiff-arm a would-be tackler, make a couple of moves, and outrun the pursuit for a long touchdown. He would actually practice moves in his head before performing them on the field.

Several weeks later Nick went out against the Holy Cross football team and racked up a record-setting 277 yards. This came as no shock to those of us who knew him. He had a vision of what he wanted to be and do before he ever saw it materialize. Nick practiced and worked hard to become what he visualized. He was not just a dreamer. He was diligent and worked toward the actualization of his vision.

Seven years had passed since we had seen each other. Our life paths had taken decidedly different directions, and I had lost track of Nick. I had trusted Christ as my Savior in 1980 and went off to Bible college in the Chicago area. As I mentioned earlier, I worked in South Chicago bringing folks to church on a bus all day on Sundays. One cold, gray Chicago evening I was in the home of two middle-aged brothers who regularly rode my bus to church. One of the brothers had lost both his legs in Vietnam. I was sitting in their modest living room waiting for them to finish preparing to go to church with us that evening. It was January 30, 1983, Super Bowl Sunday. The TV was on, and I was only half watching some of the game between the Washington Redskins and the Miami Dolphins. Suddenly number 30 for the Redskins ran onto the field, and the camera showed the name on the back of his jersey—Giaquinto.

I was taken by surprise. Since coming to Christ I had not watched much, if any, television. I deliberately did not follow what was once my god, football. I did not realize that the culmination of the vision that Nick had years earlier was coming to fruition. He had not been drafted by any professional team out of college. He was cut by the New York Giants and then by the New York Jets. He was cut from the Canadian Football League. In 1982, he finally made the Miami Dolphins but was put on waivers by them earlier in the year and was picked up by Washington. He was now playing flanker with the soon-to-be-victorious Washington Redskins in the 1983 Super Bowl. I watched just a few plays before the bus pulled up out front and it was time to go. In my heart there rose a sense of loss and regret that I had not realized my childhood dream of playing in the NFL and in a Super Bowl. We boarded our riders and began our forty-five minute trip to church.

I looked over my shoulder into the faces of the children and adults on that bus. Many of them were immigrant Mexicans who came to Chicago for work and a piece of the American dream. In too many of their cases the street gangs of South Chicago had turned that dream into a nightmare. There was the Gomez family of ten whom I had just met on Thanksgiving weekend. They recently came from Mexico and were not dressed to deal with the ruthless, relentless, and frigid winds of Chicago. I was visiting in the neighborhood, and I found their two little girls playing outside their apartment with no coats and no shoes in sub-freezing temperatures. I knocked on the door and introduced myself, and they invited me into their lives. My wife and I, along with some of our follow church workers, took the family to the Goodwill store and bought them some winter clothes.

There was little Hector, who was the only person from his family who came to church. His brother had just murdered another gang member and was going away to prison for the rest of his life. There were Roy and Rose with their little baby girl. We found out later that Roy had changed his name and was hiding from the law. There was another family of six children whose father would get drunk and use them for target practice with his BB gun. Dozens of people who needed the Lord and the compassion of His church would take that weekly ride to services with us. God broke my prideful heart that night. Tears streamed down my cheeks as God gave me a vision for my life. No, I did not see lights or hear voices, but God spoke to my heart that this was my "Super Bowl" every Sunday, and I have an audience of One.

My vision has been to reach out and help hurting people, especially those who have very little of this world's goods. I was already doing that in Chicago. I would be able to do that in some of the poverty-stricken projects of Staten Island as an associate pastor at Calvary Chapel. As a pastor at Blessed Hope Bible Church in Pennsylvania, I led our church in a mission program that helped reach people in some of the poorest countries in the world, such as Peru, Mexico, Zambia, Malawi, Tanzania, and India. We regularly helped wayward teens in Puerto Rico and America find their way to Christ and a fulfilling life. Today, I travel with Gospelink Missions, raising funds to help Christians in Africa, India, Russia, and Ukraine. This book will also help fund that vision.

Every church must have a leadership team that has a vision to accomplish the Great Commission with compassion in their hometown and in other parts of the world. The leaders must put that vision before the church people and keep the focus there without getting sidetracked. Does your church have a vision, and is it moving toward that vision with purpose?

### Thieves That Can Steal Your Vision

The patriarch Joseph, the favorite son of Jacob, had a vision for his life even as a teenaged boy. We are told about the life of Joseph in Genesis 37-50. Joseph's dreams in Genesis 37 gave him his vision from God for his future leadership of his family and the known world at the time. Three thieves could have robbed him of that vision, and yet he prevailed to see his vision fulfilled by God.

*The thief called Scorner sought to steal Joseph's dreams.* When Joseph was seventeen, he had two dreams that depicted his future as a great leader. He shared those dreams with his older brothers, who hated him and ridiculed him. Even his father, Jacob, scoffed at Joseph when he heard of the dreams (Gen. 37:1-11). This did not deter Joseph. He simply trusted what God had told him.

There are many folks, young and old, who have a vision for what they would like to do for God, but they are criticized by people. Friends and family members tell them how foolish they are or how impossible their dreams seem. More than one godly pastor has been scoffed at by unbelieving church members who did not catch his vision for the church. Just before I started Blessed Hope Bible Church, several pastors with whom I was acquainted told me that a church could never be started there. Years later, I stood in a cornfield on top of a hill on Thanksgiving Day in 1992 and asked God to give that property to our church. I shared that vision with our church family. We prayed, and God answered. The owner of the land wanted far too much money for the property and would not sell to us at first. Later, he sold us more land than we originally requested for far less. Praise the Lord! It took longer than I wanted, but God brought about the vision He had placed in my heart.

Do not let scorners steal your dreams! Keep praying for God's leadership. Stay in the Word of God and His promises, which support your God-given burden. Keep fellowship with people who are an encouragement to you and your vision. Continue to work diligently toward your goals.

*The thief called Suffering sought to steal Joseph's dream.* Joseph was not only ridiculed by his brothers but also was sold into slavery by them. Fueled by their jealousy and hatred, they first threw Joseph into a pit. The brothers were considering killing him when a caravan of Ishmaelites came along, and they opted to sell him into slavery. Joseph was taken down to Egypt and sold to the keeper of Pharaoh's prison, Potiphar. After Joseph advanced to the position of head steward in the house of Potiphar, the wife of Potiphar falsely accused Joseph of trying to rape her, because he resisted her attempt to seduce him. Joseph is sent to prison for several more years. Think about the suffering Joseph went through. He could have given up on his dreams and on God. But he did not. Almost seventeen years passed from the time Joseph had his dreams until he saw them become a reality. He stayed true to his vision, and God eventually blessed him.

How often I have seen people give up because life gets difficult. Anything worth doing for God will cost us something. Satan does not give up ground without a fight. God builds our faith and deepens our walk with Him through our trials. When God does bring our vision to fruition after much difficulty, He is given much glory. There usually is no doubting that it was God who did it.

*The thief called Sin sought to steal Joseph's dream.* Joseph was tempted to commit adultery with Potiphar's wife. If he had relented to her advances, he would no doubt have had many more privileges. After all he had been through, he could have rationalized to himself that God did not care about him. He was far from home; who would know of his actions? However, if Joseph had given into sin's temptation his relationship with God would have been harmed. Joseph was loyal to his employer and ultimately would not do this great wickedness against his God (Gen. 39:9). Many Christians have given into immorality and sold out the vision for service God has given them. I know several very gifted men of God, old and young, who have traded their spiritual legacy for a moment of lust.

Two young evangelists were as gifted as any preachers I have ever heard, and God was blessing them greatly. They both gave up those wonderful gifts for the lust of the flesh. One of those men told me that for about a year, he preached very effectively against the sin he was practicing. He said God had given him the truth that would set him free, but instead of living the truth he simply preached it to others. Let that be a sober warning to all of us, especially preachers.

God help us not to sell our God-given vision for a mess of fleshly pottage. Sin always takes us further than we want to go. It costs us more than we want to pay and keeps us longer than we want to stay.

# Blind Eyes

Blind eyes see dead skies
See only themselves, put others on shelves

Blind eyes believe all lies, death so far away
Living for the day

Blind eyes fill their life with sighs of regret
But then forget

Open eyes see bright skies, forget about themselves
Put their troubles on shelves

Open eyes reject all lies, death may come soon
But they whistle the same tune

Open eyes bring others to see the light
Know this life is a temporary fight, have no fear of death's bite

—Christal Mancari

# Loss of Blood

And without the shedding of blood is no remission [forgiveness].—Heb. 9:22

For the preaching of the cross is to them that perish foolishness; but unto us that are saved it is the power of God.—1 Cor. 1:18

Forasmuch as ye know that ye were not redeemed with corruptible things, as with silver and gold, from your vain conversation received by tradition from your fathers; But with the precious blood of Christ, as of a lamb without spot.—1 Pet. 1:18

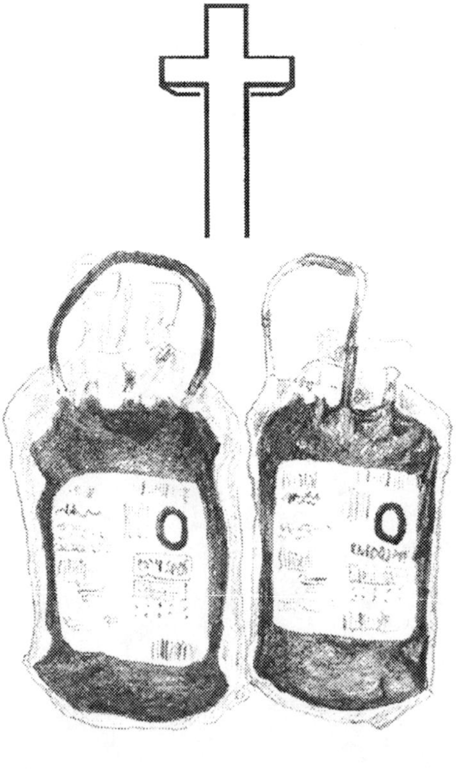

# Chapter 9

# Loss of Blood

The average adult has about five liters of blood inside of their body, coursing through their vessels, delivering essential elements, and removing harmful wastes. Without blood, the human body would stop working.

Blood is the fluid of life, transporting oxygen from the lungs to body tissue and carbon dioxide from body tissue to the lungs. Blood is the fluid of growth, transporting nourishment from digestion and hormones from glands throughout the body. Blood is the fluid of health, transporting disease-fighting substances to the tissue and waste to the kidneys.

The church we are now examining has lost almost all of its blood. The church has bled to death! This is the cause of death for many churches today. There is very little, if any, preaching on the cross of Christ. There is no longer a willingness to emphasize the shed blood of Christ for the salvation of sinners. Some modern hymn writers and publishers are taking the songs about the blood of Calvary's cross and doing away with them. This is deadly to any New Testament church. Now I am not saying that such a church cannot grow in numbers. In fact, a bigger crowd will gather because the shed blood of Christ on the cross is an offense to this world. The absence of the blood makes the presence of the unredeemed much more probable.

**Why the Cross and Blood of Christ Are an Offense**

Dying churches all over America have fallen prey to the temptation Charles H. Spurgeon described over a hundred forty years ago in London. He was concerned that many pastors had geared their services to please the lost. He said, "Many of our churches are feeding goats and starving the sheep. We must be willing to preach Christ crucified no matter the offense." The apostle Paul said to the Corinthians and the Galatians that the preaching of the cross is a stumbling block and an offense to the unbeliever (1 Cor. 1:23; Gal.5:11). The word in these verses for stumbling block and offense is the same word in the Greek text, skandalon. The trigger of a trap that snaps into action when touched is a vivid definition. Have you ever set a mousetrap and tested it by touching the little metal trigger? That is how sensitive the world is to the blood of Christ and His cross. We get our English word "scandal" from this Greek word. The cross is a scandalous object to the world. It is a source of shame. It can trigger contempt and scorn from this world's system. Why?

To the Jewish mind the cross meant disgrace. Cursed is any one who hangs on a tree, says the Law. How could the Anointed of God, Messiah, be cursed of God on the cross? It was unthinkable to the Jewish person. The cross will not allow the Law of Moses to save anyone, but it will convict us of our sin and need for the Savior of the cross. The Jewish mind would never allow, as they saw it, for Moses to be usurped by this pretentious young rabbi hanging on a tree.

To the Roman mind the cross meant the defeat of a weak enemy of the state. The Roman life was all about glorious victory. Strength of body and will were a premium in their eyes. If one did die in defeat, at least let it be in battle with honor not on a cross in shame. No Roman citizen was allowed to be put to death on a cross, because their culture so despised it.

To the Greek mind it meant a gross demeaning of man. They worshiped the myth of human perfection in body and mind. The cross was foolish and disgusting to the Hellenistic philosophy and celebration of the greatness of man's intellect and self-awareness. These were the people who gave the world Plato, Aristotle, Alexander the Great, Socrates, Homer, and Hippocrates. The cross was dismissed by them as a lesser myth.

Today some believe it to be too simple. How could faith in a despised Jewish rabbi, betrayed by His own people, judged by a corrupt Roman politician, and put to death on a Roman cross, save anyone? Simply believe in this unassuming man? The way of the cross it too simple, they say. What intelligent person would believe such a story?

Some believe it to be narrow and dogmatic. You mean to tell me that this despised, rejected, crucified, poor Jewish carpenter-turned-rabbi is the world's only hope of salvation from hell? That is far too narrow-minded and pretentious, says modern man. The Romans with their pluralistic view of religion and many gods did not like it either. My flesh wants to do things my way, but Jesus says, "I am the way, the truth and the life, no man comes to the Father but by me" (John14:6). As a matter of fact, "No man can come to the Son unless the Father draws him" (John 6:44). Even many Christians have a problem with that one.

The cross offends the notion of human ability. Man likes to think he can pull himself up by his own bootstraps. The cross says you can do nothing to save yourself. You are hopeless to even add the smallest of works to your salvation. All you can do is place all your trust in Christ and Him alone for your eternal destiny. This humbles man and guts him of his pride. "Nothing in my hands I bring, simply to Thy cross I cling," as the song goes. The ground is level at the cross for all mankind, and this offends the moralist who believes he is better than most. "Don't give me the blood and thunder of the cross, but give me the religion of ladders and levels by which I may ascend to glory" declares this modern Pharisee.

The cross offends the logic of human justice. A man, a perfectly sinless man, of royal blood, and the very Son of God, was Christ. He took on the form of a servant, despised and rejected by His own people, betrayed and abandoned by His friends. He gave up His life by laying it down as a sacrifice to His Father for the sake of those who hated Him and rejected Him. This is amazing grace!

I have three daughters and a son. Luke is my youngest child and being the only boy has certain attachments to me. I adore all my children, but he, at this juncture of my life, spends more time with me than the others. We went to pick out a Christmas tree together earlier this evening and strung up the lights. He is doing his homework in my office as I am writing these pages. Even at the age of seven, he has an interest in the things of the Lord. He has requested a meeting with me after school tomorrow to discuss some questions he has about why people are ashamed of the cross. If, and I can scarce type the words, some wicked man would take my son from our home, hurt him, and end his life, I would be devastated. Let us suppose the Virginia police captured the criminal, brought him to trial, found him guilty, and sentenced him to death. What if the judge who declared the sentence said, "I know justice demands that someone dies for this crime, but I love this murderer, so I will execute my son instead and let this criminal go home." Do you think I would rejoice over that? No! Do you think I would logically approve of that? No! It offends my sense of justice.

What Christ has done on the cross transcends any human logic or judicial system ever thought up. It is a mystery! One thing most evangelical Christians do not like is a mystery, but there are things about our God and His gospel of the cross that we may never comprehend. The believer must simply accept "But of Him are we in Christ Jesus, Who became for us wisdom from God and righteousness and sanctification and redemption that as it is written, He who glories, let us glory in the Lord" (1 Cor.1:30-31). That is why Paul said to the Galatians, "But God forbid that I should glory, save in the cross of our Lord Jesus Christ" (Gal.6:14). The cross is truly God's radical and astonishing work. Breathtaking grace!

The cross is an offense to those who do not believe. It shows the horrible wickedness of our sin because of the cost God is willing to pay for our redemption. The cross humbles the sinner and compels him to cast all his care and sin on the Lord. It is not the right or responsibility of any church to take away or diminish the offense of the cross. To take away the offense of the cross is to devalue the blood of Jesus and to take away its power.

The Lord's call in the heart of the sinner is the only way for the offense to be removed. God effectively takes that offense and turns it into the humbling power of God. The wisdom of God and the foolishness of the cross are transformed by the Holy Spirit in the heart of the sinner as the wisdom of God unto salvation. This divine work culminates in God alone getting all the glory (1 Cor. 1:18-29).

**Why Is the Blood of Christ So Precious?**

Something that is precious is costly, beloved, rare, cherished, and of great importance. Such is the blood of Christ.

* The blood of Christ redeems us; it is not corruptible and neither is our salvation (1 Pet. 1:18-19).
* The blood of Christ is a propitiation (payment) for our sin debt (Rom. 3:25; 1 John 22:2).
* The blood of Christ gives us forgiveness in God's eyes (Eph. 1:7; Col. 1:20, 22).
* The blood of Christ cleanses us in our own conscience (1 John 1:7, 9; Heb. 9:14; Rev. 12:9-11). It is one thing to have God forgive us, but it is even better when we also have minds clear of guilt. Satan tries to use our past to cripple us with guilt. We must remember that the blood of Jesus was shed for our sins whenever the accuser of the brethren, Satan, throws them in our face.
* The blood of Christ brings justification to us (Rom. 5:9).This is a legal declaration by God about all His children who have trusted the shed blood of Jesus for the remission of our sins. God considers us to be just as righteous as Jesus is.
* The blood of Christ gives us access to the throne of God (Eph. 2:13; Heb. 10:19). We are by nature spiritually far from God and have no clear access to pray at the throne of grace. The blood of Jesus tore down the veil between us and our heavenly Father and has given us admittance into the Holy of Holies (Luke 23:45).

There is a story told of Napoleon Bonaparte as he viewed a map showing the areas of his conquest. He pointed to England, which was a relatively small, red island on that map. Napoleon moaned in frustration, "If not for that one red blotch I would rule the world." Satan could make a similar claim, looking at a world he could have completely ruled if not for the one blood-stained hill called Calvary.

It was there on the cross that Jesus shed His blood to ransom His people and defeat Satan.

**There Is Power in the Blood**

Would you be free from your burden of sin?
There's power in the blood, power in the blood;
Would you o'er evil a victory win?
There's wonderful power in the blood.

Would you be free from your passion and pride?
There's power in the blood, power in the blood;
Come for cleansing to Calvary's tide.
There's wonderful power in the blood.

Would you be whiter, much whiter than snow?
There's power in the blood, power in the blood;
Sin stains are lost in its life-giving flow.
There's wonderful power in the blood.

Would you do service for Jesus, your King?
There's power in the blood, power in the blood;
Would you live daily His praises to sing?
There's wonderful power in the blood.

There is power, power, wonder-working power
In the blood of the Lamb.
There is power, power, wonder-working power
In the precious blood of the Lamb.

—Lewis E. Jones

The church that does not value the cross of Christ and His shed blood will be anemic and weak. There is power in the preaching of the cross, and we should never outgrow the mystery and love of the cross. We can be sure that Satan will try everything he can to distract us from the preaching of the cross, because it is the cross that dooms his wicked efforts to destroy God's kingdom. We also consider the world to be no friend to the preaching of the cross; hence it will seek to divert the church's efforts to magnify the shed blood of Jesus on the cross.

> And they sang a new song, saying, Thou art worthy to take the book, and to open the seals thereof: for thou wast slain, and hast redeemed us to God by thy blood out of every kindred, and tongue, and people, and nation.—Rev. 5:9

# Alas! And Did My Savior Bleed

Alas! And did my Savior bleed,
And did my Sovereign die?
Would He devote that sacred head
for such a worm as I?

Was it for sins that I have done
He suffered on the tree?
Amazing pity! Grace unknown!
And love beyond degree!

Well might the sun in darkness hide,
And shut His glories in,
When God, the mighty Maker, died
For man the creature's sin.

Thus might I hide my blushing face
While His dear cross appears:
Dissolve my heart in thankfulness,
And melt mine eyes to tears.

But drops of grief can ne'er repay
The debt of love owe;
Here, Lord, I give myself away;
'Tis all that I can do.

—Isaac Watts

# Untamed Tongues Set on Fire

Death and life are in the power of the tongue.
—Prov. 18:21

And the tongue is a fire, a world of iniquity: so is the tongue among our members, that it defileth the whole body, and setteth on fire the course of nature; and it is set on fire of hell. But the tongue can no man tame; it is an unruly evil, full of deadly poison.—James 5:6,8

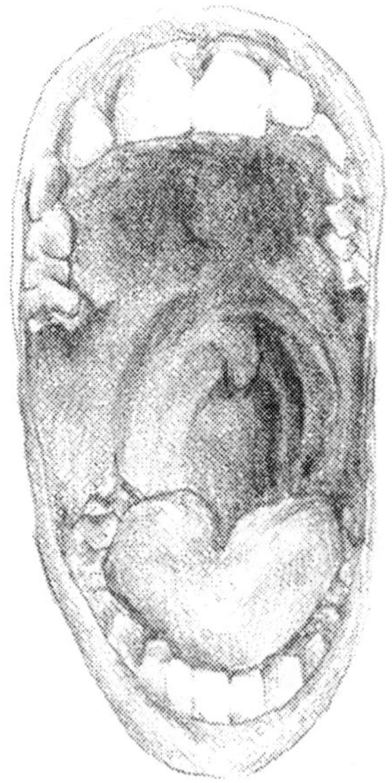

# Chapter 10

# Untamed Tongues Set on Fire

Problems with the tongue may include pain, hairy appearance, unusual color, unusual smoothness, swelling, mouth ulcers, white lining, a split or groove in the tongue (fissure), cobblestone appearance, or positioning off to one side.

The tongue is composed mainly of muscles. It is covered with a mucous membrane. Small bumps (papillae) cover the upper surface of the tongue. Between the papillae are the taste buds, which provide the sense of taste. In addition to taste, the tongue functions in moving food to aid chewing and swallowing, and it is important in speech.

The tongue of this dead church has been examined and found to have burn marks all over it. This tongue has set many fires and finally burns itself to death. We have also found residue of deadly poison on this tongue. Justin Martyr said, "By examining the tongue of the patient, physicians find out the disease of the body, and philosophers the diseases of the mind." The tongue is the ambassador of the heart.

You might recall as a child hearing this saying: "Sticks and stones may break my bones, but words will never hurt me." How untrue are those words! The truth is that the greatest source of hurt for most of us has been the words someone has launched our way. Many churches and their people have been mortally wounded by the tongues of gossips and angry people. If a church is to maintain a healthy body life, the congregation needs to have their tongues under the control of the Holy Spirit. Most church splits are nothing but a "war of words."

**Tips on Taming our Tongues**

I have purposely used an abundance of Scripture in this section, because only God the Holy Spirit can control our unruly tongues (James 3:8). Let the Lord's truth wash out our mouth as only He can.

* *Remember that words can harm or heal*:

"There is that speaketh like the piercings of a sword: but the tongue of the wise is health" (Prov. 12:18).

"Heaviness in the heart of a man maketh it stoop: but a good word maketh it glad" (Prov. 12:25).

"A soft answer turneth away wrath; but grievous words stir up anger" (Prov. 15:1).

"The tongue of the wise useth knowledge aright: but the mouth of fools poureth out foolishness" (Prov. 15:2).

"A word fitly spoken is like apples of gold in pictures of silver" (Prov. 25:11).

It is far better to choose what you say than to just say what you choose. Many church splits and broken friendships have been caused by hasty and harsh words that have deeply hurt others. How very careful we should be with what and how we say things. We can all offend with our words. Be a healer with your words!

* *Speak the truth in love*:

"But speaking the truth in love, may grow up in Him in all things, which is the head, even Christ: Wherefore putting away lying, speak every man truth with his neighbor: for we are members one of another" (Eph. 4:15, 25).

God does not muzzle us from expressing His truth, but we must always have love as our motive. We should not wield the truth simply to put someone in their place, to justify ourselves, or to win an argument for pride's sake. Many of the religious debates that take place among people within and without the body of Christ tend to be about lifting up egos and not loving edification, especially among those evangelicals who have entered into the political arena in the recent years. Their rhetoric has been less than loving and God-honoring. We should certainly be able to disagree without being disagreeable. A bit of love is the only bit that will put a bridle on the tongue. "Let all bitterness, and wrath, and anger, and clamour, and evil speaking, be put away from you, with all malice" (Eph. 4:31).

* *Speak with grace and edifying words not attacking and corrupting words*:

"Let no corrupt communication proceed out of your mouth, but that which is good to the use of edifying, that it may minister grace unto the hearers" (Eph. 4:29).

It is important to keep our words sweet, for we may later have to eat them. Wouldn't we have far better churches if we all sought to find something positive to say every time we attended services? I challenge you to say something encouraging to five different people every occasion you have to be at the church—not flattery (false compliments used to manipulate people) but honest praise about something good concerning their character. You will make more friends (Prov. 18:24), and people will more often become what we praise (Prov. 27:21).

Some people in the church tend to talk just to be heard. Remember the warning of Solomon: "In a multitude of words there wanteth not [no lack of] sin: but he that refrains his lips is wise" (Prov. 10:19). There is much back and forth banter among church members that crosses a line of suitable speech for Christians. Humor at the expense of another's feelings can be hurtful and damaging to the spirit of unity in the church. "Neither filthiness, nor foolish talking, nor jesting, which are not convenient [not fitting]: but rather giving of thanks" (Eph. 5:4).

* *Listen before we speak*:

"He that answereth a matter before he heareth it, it is a folly and a shame unto him" (Prov. 18:13)

Take time to listen before we react to people: "Let every man be swift to hear and slow to speak" (James 1:19). It would be far better to leave people wondering why we did not speak than why we did.

Before we make up our minds that we are right about something, we need to make sure we hear everyone's side (Prov. 18:17). I have been in many situations as a pastor and a parent when I thought I knew what had transpired, but I was glad that I waited to hear the other person's perspective. My understanding was greatly improved, and I was able to give far better counsel. We need to listen before we leap to conclusions.

Also, show that you are really listening. There is nothing more irritating to someone than to have us looking around them or through them while they are speaking to us. This goes on all around the church every Sunday. Some people glad-hand their way around a room as if they are running for political office. Stop, look the person in the eyes, and listen actively.

* *It takes some time and wisdom to discover the meaning behind a person's words. Good listeners are at a premium and will never lack friends.*

"Counsel in the heart of man is like deep water; but a man of understanding will draw it out" (Prov. 20:5). This text tells us that if we want to truly know what is in the heart of a person we must listen not only to the words spoken but also those that are unspoken. We have all asked a family member or friend a question such as "Are you all right?" And the reply is a half-hearted shrug: "Sure." What they mean is, "I am not all right, but help me to tell you about it."

We are all too busy to listen and get to know people. No matter how big the church is we can feel lonely if we do not make a connection with someone. I appreciate the fact that churches are trying to use small groups to get people to know each other. I am concerned that they are cutting into the time that could be spent teaching the Bible, but we all need fellowship. Perhaps churches could stop keeping families so busy with so many activities and encourage people to develop meaningful friendships in Christ. Some bigger churches are like machines churning along, scooping up people, and spitting them out if they do not quite fit the mold. After a while it becomes nothing more than a numbers game.

* *Pray for God to help us with our words*:

"Set a watch, O Lord, before my mouth; keep the door of my lips" (Ps. 141:3).

"The Lord God hath given me the tongue of the learned, that I should know how to speak a word in season to him that is weary; He wakeneth morning by morning, He wakeneth my ear to hear as the learned" (Is. 50:4). Remember, we speak not just with our words but also with our body language, our facial expressions, and our tone of voice. Ask God to teach us godly communication in all these areas.

The psalmist prayed, "Let the words of my mouth, and the meditation of my heart, be acceptable in thy sight, O LORD, my strength, and my redeemer" (Ps. 19:14).

Some of the most sobering comments in the Bible regarding our words are these: "But I say unto you, That every idle word that men shall speak, they shall give account thereof in the day of judgment" (Matt. 12:36).

* *Keep our disagreements with others confidential.*

"A perverse man sows strife, and a whisperer [gossip] separateth chief friends" (Prov. 16:28).

"The words of a talebearer are as wounds, and they go down into the innermost parts of the belly" (Prov. 18:8).

"Debate thy cause with thy neighbor himself; and discover not a secret to another" (Prov. 25:9)

"Speak not evil one of another, brethren" (James 4:11).

A big problem in churches is that disagreements and offenses are multiplied through the fellowship because of gossip. One party or both parties in a dispute tell other people about it, and people start to take sides. Before you know it, there is a full-blown feud taking place, and the church is the battleground. Offenses will come and go in our lives, but we do not need to compound the damage done to the church by spreading the dispute to others. A molehill becomes a mountain because gossips keep shoveling the dirt. Galatians 5:15 says, "But if you bite and devour one another, take heed that ye be not consumed one of another." Corrie ten Boom said, "Gossip leads to criticism, and criticism kills love."

May God keep the tongues of the church occupied with praising the Lord and proclaiming the gospel. We would be far less likely to be found doing what we should not, if we were more diligently engaged doing what we ought! Charles Wesley's great hymn "O For a Thousand Tongues to Sing" often reminds me how I should be employing my tongue most constructively.

## O For a Thousand Tongues to Sing

O for a thousand tongues to sing
My great Redeemer's Praise,
The glories of my God and King,
The triumphs of His grace.

Jesus! The name that charms our fears,
That bids our sorrows cease,
'Tis music in the sinner's ears,
'Tis life and health and peace.

He breaks the power of cancelled sin,
He sets the prisoner free;
His blood can make the foulest clean;
His blood availed for me.

Hear Him, ye deaf; His praise, ye dumb,
Your loosened tongues employ;
Ye blind, behold your Savior come;
And leap, ye lame for joy.

My gracious Master and my God,
Assist me to proclaim,
To spread thro' all the earth abroad,
The honors of Thy name.

—Charles Wesley

# Unbending Knees and Unholy Hands

And when he had thus spoken, he kneeled down, and prayed with them all.—Acts 20:36

Pray without ceasing.—1 Thess. 5:17

I will therefore that men pray every where, lifting up holy hands, without wrath and doubting.—1 Tim. 2:8

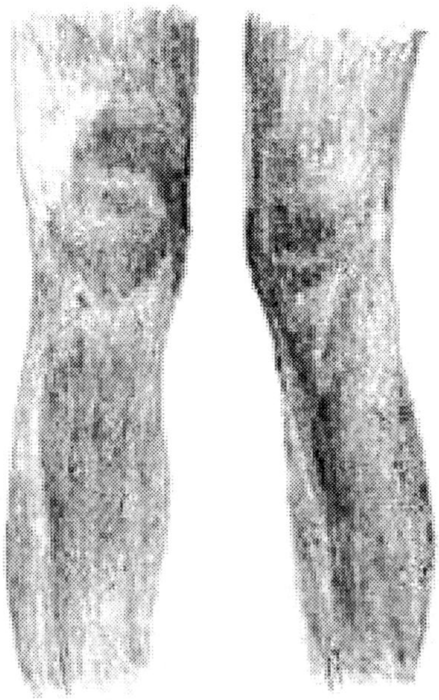

## Chapter 11

# Unbending Knees and Unholy Hands

Each year, millions of Americans limp into doctors' offices and emergency rooms with knee pain. Often, the pain is the result of an injury such as a ruptured ligament or torn cartilage. But certain medical conditions can also bring you to your knees, including arthritis, gout, and infections.

Depending on the type and severity of damage, knee pain can be a minor annoyance, causing an occasional twinge when you kneel down or exercise strenuously. Or it can lead to severe discomfort and disability. For a college or professional football or basketball player a knee injury is one of the most dreaded. Torn cartilage or ligaments usually are season-ending and sometimes career-ending injuries. If the knee is not operating correctly, you cannot run, and therefore you cannot play.

My freshman year at the University of Connecticut I had a roommate who tore ligaments in his knee playing football. He had an operation, and his knee was in a cast for several weeks. His playing season was over, but that was only the beginning of his problems. He could not bend his knee, so he had trouble walking with crutches. He needed help carrying his books and his food tray. Simply getting dressed became a challenging adventure for him. Topping everything off we had an ice storm, and the electricity was knocked out for a couple of days. We lived on the sixth floor of our dorm, and the elevator was not working. Several of us had to practically carry him down a dark stairwell to get to classes and meals for a couple of days. And this was not so easy since he was 6 feet 2 inches and well over two hundred pounds. That unbending knee caused more hassles and difficulties than we could imagine.

Unbending knees for the Christian is a metaphor for a lack of prayer. Prayer is the most spiritual thing any Christian can do. Without a prayer life the church and her people are seriously injured and handicapped. They are in critical condition before the enemy of their souls, Satan. The devil does not fear us or any of our fleshly plans. The only one he fears is God. "Satan trembles when he sees the weakest saint upon his knees," said William Cowper. Therefore, we must have the Lord involved in everything we do personally and as a church.

The autopsy of the dead church has revealed to us that this church has stiff knee joints. These knees have rarely been bent in prayer. This church has been involved with the work of God but has relegated God to a spectator.

Years ago, Yankees Hall of Fame catcher Yogi Berra was playing in a close game. A batter from the other team came up to the plate with the score tied and two outs in the bottom of the ninth inning. The opposing player stepped into the batter's box and made the sign of the cross, as many Catholics do. Yogi was a Catholic, too, so he leaned forward, brushed off home plate with his glove, and said to the pious batter, "Why don't we just let God watch this game?" Many Christians and churches are content to have God merely in attendance. Oh, maybe they will have Him throw out the first pitch, in the same way they pray before meals or to open up the service. But sadly, prayer has been pushed aside as perfunctory tradition—and along with it, God's power.

### What Some Prominent People Have Said about Prayer

"All the Christian virtues are locked up in the word prayer."
—Charles Haddon Spurgeon

"Certain thoughts are prayers. There are moments when, whatever be the attitude of the body, the soul is on its knees."

—Victor Hugo

"I have been driven many times to my knees by the overwhelming conviction that I had nowhere else to go. My own wisdom, and that of all about me, seemed insufficient for the day."

—Abraham Lincoln

"Our prayers lay the track down by which God's power can come. Like a mighty locomotive, his power is irresistible, but it cannot reach us without rails." —Watchman Nee

"Prayer is a shield to the soul, a sacrifice to God, and a scourge to Satan." —John Bunyan

"Prayer is the easiest and hardest of all things; the simplest and the sublimest; the weakest and the most powerful; its results lie outside the range of human possibilities; they are limited only by the omnipotence of God." —E. M. Bounds

"The principle exercise of the child of God is to pray, for in this they give a true proof of their faith." —John Calvin

"The Christian on his knees sees more than the philosopher on his tiptoe. I'd rather be able to pray than to be a great preacher; Jesus Christ never taught his disciples how to preach, but only how to pray." —D. L. Moody

"Prayer should cover the whole of life, life in all its extent and detail." —John Murray

"We are too busy to pray, and so we are too busy to have power. We have a great deal of activity, but we accomplish little; many services but few conversions; much machinery but few results. Prayer is the key that unlocks all the storehouses of God's infinite grace and

power. All that God is, and all that God has, is at the disposal of prayer."
—R. A. Torrey

"We are ill-taught if we look for results only in the earthlies when we pray. A praying saint performs far more havoc among the unseen forces of darkness than we have the slightest notion of."
—Oswald Chambers

"More things are wrought by prayer than this world dreams of."
—Alfred, Lord Tennyson

"Men who know their God are before anything else men who pray, and the first point where their zeal and energy for God's glory come to expression is in their prayers."
—J. I. Packer

"The one concern of the devil is to keep Christians from praying. He fears nothing from prayerless studies, prayerless works, and prayerless religion. He laughs at our toil, mocks at wisdom, but trembles when we pray."
—Samuel Chadwick

"Prayer, with thanksgiving, being one special part of religious worship, is by God required of all men: and that it may be accepted, it is to be made in the name of the Son, by the power of the help of the Holy Spirit, according to His will, with understanding, reverence, humility, fervency, faith, love, and perseverance; and, if vocal, in a known tongue."
—Westminster Confession of Faith

"Moreover as for me, God forbid that I should sin against the LORD in ceasing to pray for you."
—Sam. 12:23

**Thou Art Coming to a King**

Large petitions with thee bring;
For his grace and power are such
None can ever ask too much.

—John Newton

## What the Bible Says about Prayer

The power and necessity of prayer is beyond any person's ability to totally comprehend and express. While contemplating these preceding comments, does it not seem a pity that so few Christians or churches really learn to earnestly pray? Let us exam more closely what the Bible says about prayer.

Prayer is the born-again (regenerated) believer communicating with God the Creator and Redeemer of all heaven and earth (Prov. 15:8, 29; Ps. 145:18; Matt. 6:6-9). This prayer presupposes that there is a God who hears, cares, and is omnipotent (all-powerful); He has the ability to answer any request in a fashion He deems suitable (Prov. 16:1, 9; 21:1).

The requisites to prayer are sincerity (Matt. 6:7), reverence (Ps. 89:7), humility (Luke 18:13), fervency (James 5:16), and faith (James 1:6-7). Prayer consists of asking (Matt. 7:7-8), confession (1 John 1:9), adoration (Psalm 8), and thanksgiving (Col. 1:3; Phil. 4:6). Types of prayer are inward and silent (1 Sam. 1:13; Neh. 2:4), audible (Ps. 5:2-3), private (Matt. 6:6; 14:22-23), and public (Acts 20:36). The place for prayer is everywhere (1 Tim. 2:8). For whom are we to pray? Everyone (1 Tim. 2:1)! This includes our enemies (Matt. 5:44). "There is nothing that makes us love a man so much as praying for him," said William Law. How many churches have prayed for the terrorists in the Middle East?

The normal protocol for addressing God in prayer is to the Father (John 16:23), in the name of the Son (John 14:14), and in the power of the Holy Spirit (Jude 20). The different postures of prayer are standing (Mark 11:25), kneeling (Luke 22:41), looking to heaven (John 17:1), lying prostrate on the ground (Matt. 26:39), and even hanging on the cross (Luke 23:42). Erwin Lutzer has said, "Although posture is not important, I find that I am able to express my dependence better on my knees, a sign of our helplessness apart from the divine enablement." In reality, the position of the body is not as important as the condition of the heart (Ps. 66:18-20).

## Jesus and the Early Church at Prayer

Jesus is our prototype of prayer. Our Lord began His ministry with prayer (Luke 3:21) and continued His ministry with prayer (Mark

1:35-38). The ministry of Jesus counted on prayer (Luke 5:15-16), and even His miracles were consummated by prayer (Matt. 14:14-23). Many churches call for prayer meetings when they have an important request of the Lord. But how many have held a prayer meeting after God answers their prayer? Jesus chose His twelve apostles after spending the night in prayer (Luke 6:12-13). Sounds like a great plan before a church calls a pastor or a pastor hires a staff member.

The Lord's earthly ministry concluded in prayer. We find Him sweating drops of blood in the garden, praying earnestly (Matt. 26:36-41; Luke 23:34). One of the greatest examples of earnest prayer is found in Daniel 9. Daniel cries out no less than ten times, "O, Lord!" Jesus our Lord ever lives to make intercession for His people (Heb. 7:24-26). Jesus, the perfectly sinless, virgin-born Son of God, prayed all the time. We need to be constant in prayer as well (1 Thess. 5:18).

The early church gives us more illustrations of prayer. They were steadfast in prayer (Acts 2:42) and prayed for boldness in preaching (Acts 4:29). Our churches today certainly need prayer for boldness and power as we put on God's armor (Eph. 6:18). We need to pray as the early church prayed for the deliverance of Peter from governmental opposition (Acts 12:5-19). The church needs to pray for and send out missionaries from their midst as did the early church (Acts 13:1-3). It has been said of James (half-brother of our Lord), the head of the community in Jerusalem, that the skin of his knees was as hard as a camel's from constantly praying and that he could pray for days.

Jesus taught His disciples how to pray (Matt. 6:9-13), and He taught them to pray by example by praying morning, noon, and night. He certainly practiced what He preached. We will briefly examine this pattern for prayer, remembering it was just that, a pattern. It was never meant to be a rote reciting of words to gain favor with God. There is a vast difference between saying prayers and praying. The Lord warns against praying with vain repetition, as the heathen do (Matt. 6:7).

The Lord begins with "Our Father," which denotes our standing as a child of God. We must be part of the family of God. All men are related together as creatures to their Creator (Mal. 2:10; Acts 17:24-26). However, there is another relationship that divides the human race spiritually. Either God, through the redemptive work of Christ Jesus, is our Father (John 1:12-13; 1 John 3:9), or we are still in our sin and our father is the devil (John 8:44; 1 John 3:10). The only time Jesus did not call God His Father was at the moment Jesus hung on the cross with our sins on Him. At that instant Jesus cried, "My God, My God, why hast Thou forsaken Me?" The title "Father" speaks of His close and caring relationship with us. Father speaks of One to be honored, respected, and obeyed. It also reminds us that we are part of a family that the Lord is committed to care for, and our prayer request will be dealt with in light of the family's needs and not just our perceived needs.

"Who art in heaven" speaks of God's perspective of eternity. He is not trapped in time with our limited view, or in "life under the sun" as Solomon called it in the poetic book of Ecclesiastes. This eternal perspective gives far more insight as to what our true needs might be and how they should be met.

"Hallowed be Thy name" reminds us of the real priority of prayer—that God's name be glorified. How will God's name be most greatly magnified? God's names are many in the Old Testament; each one emphasizes a different aspect or attribute of God. Jehovah-jireh means the "Lord has supplied." What a name to contemplate when we need Him to provide through prayer! Jehovah-shalom means the "Lord of Peace." Are we ever in need of peace? The disciples knew many of the Old Testament names for God, and these titles would have come to their recollection when Jesus said that the Lord's name (essentially, His character) should be hallowed (reverenced). As we think on the character of God, our faith is increased and our motivation to pray enhanced.

"Thy kingdom come" speaks of the rule and the reign of God through Jesus the Son in the hearts of people (Mark 1:14-15; Luke 17:20-21; John 3:3; Rom. 14:17; 1 Cor. 4:20). This is a prayer for the conversions of sinners and for Jesus to come into their heart to reign as Lord and Savior. It is also a prayer for consecration of our own lives to be more fully committed to His kingdom and its sanctifying work in our lives. Finally, as an additional application, it is a prayer of longing for the coming earthly kingdom that the Lord will set up in the future for a thousand years (Revelation 20). This is reflected in the final words in the Bible, which are a prayer: "Even so, come, Lord Jesus" (Rev. 22:20-21).

"Thy will be done on earth as it is in heaven" speaks of two aspects of the will of God. It is an earnest plea for a holy resolve to do the perceptive (revealed commands of God in His Word) will of God (Phil. 2:13; 1 John 2:17). We need to pray that God would instruct and enlighten us with the Bible's precepts so we may understand His will. We need His wisdom to apply His will. We need His grace to obey His will. "Prayer should be your steering wheel not your spare tire," said Corrie ten Boom.

Secondly, it is a plea for a holy resignation to the will of God, the secret decrees of God, especially those that are dark and difficult (Deut. 29:29; Rom. 8:28; Eph. 1:11). God is sovereign (complete ruler, almighty) over every atom. There is "not one maverick molecule" (coined by R.C. Sproul) in this whole universe over which God does not have ultimate control. Yes, man is free but not as free as God. The patriarch Joseph acknowledged God's awesome ability to take man's volitional actions, even wicked ones, and turn them into something that would have a good outcome. After he was reunited with his brothers, who had sold him into slavery, Joseph said, "But as for you, ye thought evil [man's will] against me; but God meant [God's will] it unto good, to bring to pass, as it is this day, to save much people alive" (Gen. 50:20). Prayer is used as a tool in our sanctifying process to be more aligned with the purposes of God. Prayer is used as a means to carry out God's sovereign purposes and plans. Can we pray those trusting words "Thy will be done" and know He can and will do what is best?

Evangelist D. L. Moody was right when he said, "Prayer does not mean that I am to bring God down to my thoughts and my purposes, and bend his government according to my foolish, silly, and sometimes sinful notions. Prayer means that I am to be raised up into feeling, into union and design with him; that I am to enter into his counsel and carry out his purpose fully." Leonard Ravenhill concurred: "Prayer is not an argument with God to persuade Him to move things our way, but an exercise by which we are enabled by his Spirit to move ourselves His way." The great missionary to China, Hudson Taylor, said it this way, "I used to ask God to help me. Then I asked if I might help Him. I ended up asking Him to do His work through me."

"On earth as it is in heaven" reminds us that there is only one will in heaven and that is God's will. There, God's perceptive will is understood by all, obeyed by all, all the time. Every being in heaven has an eternal view on every circumstance that arises, so they have no problem with God's decrees. Because we do not have that eternal view, we must have faith in the God we know from Scripture to always do what is right. Billy Graham's wife, Ruth, has said, "God has not always answered my prayers. If He had, I would have married the wrong man twice."

"Give us this day our daily bread" speaks of God's design to have His children seek their daily sustenance from His hand. A daily awareness of our dependence on the Lord is the attitude that He seeks from His people. He gives us the power to make wealth (Deut. 8:18). Many churches and Americans have become like the Israelites of Jeremiah's day. In Jeremiah 2, God rebukes the people for having turned their backs on Him after He led them from Egypt and through the desert into the Promised Land. When they had very little, they were closer to the Lord, but when they felt self-sufficient, they strayed from the Lord.

When I was pastoring Blessed Hope Bible Church, I would often remind the congregation to remember where we had come from and how God had graciously blessed us. We grew and went from a house church to a rented building and finally purchased a new building. I was burdened that we not lose focus on who had led us in the leaner years and was still the One we needed. We should never forget the goodness of the Lord and our daily need of His care. We never get too big for God.

"And forgive us our debts as we forgive others" speaks of our need to keep short accounts with God and others. Too often we allow sin to build up in our lives rather than confessing and repenting daily. We also need to take inventory of our relationships within the body of Christ. We cannot be right with God and wrong with our brother or sister in Christ. If two of my children have an unresolved issue with each other, then they are not completely in harmony with me, their father. I am hurt if they are not right with each other, and I will make efforts to move them toward reconciliation.

"And lead us not into temptation [trials] but deliver us from evil [the evil one]" is a request that we not have trials that would cause us to give into the temptation of the devil. Job and Peter both had such trials that Satan sought to take advantage of, but God makes a way for us to escape (1 Cor. 10:13). If we are honest about escaping the traps of sin, God will make a way for us to be victorious.

"For Thine is the kingdom, and the power, and the glory forever" brings us full circle to what it is all about. God is the preeminent One. He is the parent, He is the priority, He has the program; it is His plan and His provision. He provides the pardon and our protection. He is to be glorified!

**Scriptural Supplications for Sinners and Soulwinners**

Take Paul's prayers of Ephesians 1:16-20; 3:14-19; Colossians 1:9-11 and pray them earnestly for your family members and friends.

Here are some prayers to pray for the lost people on your prayer list. Place the name of the person you are praying for in the blank space.

Father, please draw (__________) to Christ (John 6:44).

Reprove (__________) of sin, Father, by the Holy Spirit (John 16:8).

Father, I pray for (__________) to be saved (Rom. 10:1).

Father, open (__________) eyes and heart to salvation (Act 16:14; 2 Cor. 4:3-6).

Father, please grant (__________) faith and repentance so they can know the truth and be free from the devil's snare (2 Tim. 2:25-26).

Lord, please give me boldness and clarity when I speak the gospel (Eph. 6:19).

Oh Lord, please give me open doors to speak for You (Col. 4:3-4).

Oh Lord, may Your Word have free course to be spoken, and may You give me favor with those in authority. Remove all hindrances to the gospel (2 Thess. 3:1-4).

### Hindrance to Prayer

A husband and wife relationship that is not right will hurt the prayer life of that family and church (1 Pet. 3:7). The divorce rate within the church today is as bad as it is in the world. Families are breaking up, and many of those that stay together are in bad shape. Well, if the family is crippled in their prayer life, it will naturally hurt the church. Many of our churches are burdened down with the attack on their families. Even many of our pastors' homes are in deep trouble. I recently taught a family-life class, and I was appalled at how far from the biblical pattern most families in our churches are.

I once mentioned that as a general principal I would not marry a couple who had been living together unless they moved out and repented of their fornication. One lady called me and kept me on the phone for an hour, letting me know how graceless I was to suggest such a thing. She also informed me that I used too many scriptures when teaching about the family. I could go on with more rather outrageous ideas she had, but you get my point. People in our churches often want psychology or sociology instead of good old-fashioned Bible theology. Many of our families in the church are not on praying ground, and that hurts the whole body of Christ.

Another hindrance to prayer is our relationship to other believers (Matt. 5:23-24). Before we have the path cleared to the altar of prayer, we need to get right with those who have an offense with us. Most issues in the church today are brushed under the proverbial rug and never dealt with in a biblical manner. Churches are so eager to add new wallets to their church rolls that they hardly challenge someone transferring from another church. They should be sure that they left the previous church on Christian terms with the former pastor and congregation, with no unresolved bitterness or offense. There are far too many people being offended and running down the street to join another church before they make it right. Church discipline has all but disappeared in the church of America.

Finally, the Bible tells us to lift up holy hands in prayer (1 Tim. 2:8). This lifting up of holy hands is a metaphor for a morally clean life (Ps. 66:18). The word "holy" here means unpolluted or unstained. The basis for an effective prayer life is a righteous life (James 5:16). I am very sad today when I see church after church with absolutely no standard of propriety. The pastors have to apologize for encouraging folks to dress decently. There is no sense of decorum and respect for authority—parental or church. I am so weary of hearing people say, "Well, Jesus loves them just they way they are." Yes, Jesus does love and accept us just the way we are, but He loves us too much to allow us to stay the way we are. He changes us into new creations (2 Cor. 5:17).

The great preacher of old, John Owens, wrote a sermon about the two most damning delusions of the church in England three hundred fifty years ago. The first damning delusion was that some people felt they were fit for heaven without the new birth. Baptism and church membership were all they really needed. They had never been born again and saw no need to be so (John 3:3). Most of us would certainly agree that those people are in trouble, for Scripture teaches that we must be born again! The second, and equally as damning a delusion, was that some people insisted that they had the new birth without a changed life. They had given Jesus an intellectual tip of the hat as they passed by but saw no need to get too serious about this new life in Christ. They did not want to seem too radical about this Jesus. To believe that God has saved a person from the guilt of their sin, without saving them from sin's dominion and power over their heart, is to contradict the Scriptures (Titus 2:14).

We are to be holy as He is holy (1 Pet. 1:13-15), leaving the lust of our former life. We are saved from the penalty of sin. We are being saved from the power of sin through sanctification (Rom. 8:29). We shall be saved from the presence of sin when glorified in heaven (1 John 3:1-3). Jesus said that if we love Him, we will keep His commandments (John 14:15). One major reason the churches are in trouble is because we have no power in prayer, and we have no power in prayer because we are not a holy people! You might be reading this and thinking I am condoning some kind of pharisaical legalism, and therefore you can just brush it aside. But if you are a pastor or if you have been a Christian for more than five years, you know that the American church, in general, is not holy! We are not a holy church! Every great revival in America began with effective prayer. Effective prayer comes from holy people (2 Chron. 7:14; James 5:16). God help us to become a holy people that we might be a powerful people in prayer!

# Sweet Hour of Prayer

Sweet hour of prayer, sweet hour of prayer,
That calls me from a world of care,
And bids me at my Father's throne,
Make all my wants and wishes known:

In seasons of distress and grief,
My soul has often found relief
And often escaped the tempter's snare
By thy return, sweet hour of prayer.

Sweet hour of prayer, sweet hour of prayer,
Thy wings shall my petition bear,
To Him whose truth and faithfulness,
Engage the waiting soul to bless:

And since He bids me seek His face,
Believe His Word, and trust His grace,
I'll cast on Him my every care,
And wait for thee, sweet hour of prayer.

—William W. Walford

# Ugly Feet

How then shall they call on him in whom they have not believed? And how shall they believe in him of whom they have not heard? And how shall they hear without a preacher? And how shall they preach, except they be sent? as it is written, How beautiful are the feet of them that preach the gospel of peace, and bring glad tidings of good things!—Rom. 10:14-15

How beautiful upon the mountains are the feet of him that bringeth good tidings, that publisheth peace; that bringeth good tidings of good, that publisheth salvation; that saith unto Zion, Thy God reigneth!—Isa. 52:7

# Chapter 12

# Ugly Feet

*Feet Facts*

As we conclude our autopsy of the dead church we have moved all the way down to the feet, and their appearance is, quite frankly, very ugly. Three out of four Americans experience serious foot problems in their lifetime, which is about the same ratio of churches that have spiritual foot problems. The foot contains twenty-six bones, thirty-three joints, one hundred seven ligaments and nineteen muscles. One quarter of all the bones in the human body are down in your feet. When these bones are out of alignment, so is the rest of the body. There are two hundred fifty thousand sweat glands in a pair of feet. Believe it or not, these sweat glands can excrete as much as a half-pint of moisture a day.

Only a small percentage of the population is born with foot problems. Most newly born Christians start with beautiful feet; they are delighted to tell others about the gospel. It is neglect and apathy that bring on problems. Your feet mirror your general health. Conditions such as arthritis, diabetes, and nerve and circulatory disorders can show their initial symptoms in the feet, so foot ailments can be your first sign of more serious medical problems.

Like our physical feet, the feet of a church can tell us much about its health. The feet are a metaphor for the church's evangelistic and missionary efforts, as mentioned in Romans 10:14-15. The dead church we are examining has very ugly feet, because it has not been about the business of bringing the Good News to all people.

The average person takes eight thousand to ten thousand steps a day, which adds up to about 115,000 miles over a lifetime. That is enough to go around the circumference of the earth four times. However, the average church cannot get most of its members' feet to take them around the block once to tell their neighbors about the gospel of Jesus Christ.

In order to better understand the text that we began this chapter with, please take a brief journey with me back to ancient Greece, circa 490 B.C. King Darius I of Persia is determined to conquer Greece proper, to secure his western frontier and lay the groundwork for Persia's expansion into Europe. This expedition resulted in the Battle of Marathon, perhaps the single most important battle in Greek history. Had the Athenians lost, Greece would have eventually come under the control of the Persians, and the subsequent culture and accomplishments of the Greeks would probably not have taken the form they did. The Athenian army, led by their great general, Miltiades, was outnumbered three to one. His superior strategy, however, won the battle, and they routed the Persian Army. After the battle, General Miltiades sent a young soldier, Phaedippas, to take word back over the mountain to the city of Athens. He ran the entire distance, 42.192 kilometers (twenty-six miles), shouting "Nike!" (victory) and fell dead of exhaustion. In memory of this event the marathon run has been included among the contests since the first contemporary Olympic Games.

This event is similar to that pictured in Isaiah 52:7. The messenger is told to run to the cities surrounding the area and proclaim victory! His feet are said to be beautiful as seen by those who are awaiting word of the battle, because the runner's feet are not dragging along as one who is defeated. Instead, he has the "happy feet" of one bringing glad news of victory. The apostle Paul picks up this prophetic passage, which anticipates the Lord's millennial reign, in Isaiah 52:7 and applies it in Romans 10:14-15 to the proclamation of the gospel of God's grace in the church age. The church and her people are the messengers who are to run with the good news of the gospel. We are to be the ones with beautiful, happy feet letting people know that our God reigns!

## Churches with Ugly, Frozen Feet

When I was a young teenage boy, I had a newspaper stand outside in the parking lot of our Catholic church on Sunday mornings. After each mass, I would sell the Sunday paper to people as they came out of church. Actually, it was a rather nice little job except when the winter months came and it got cold and snowy. I remember having a very warm coat, but my feet would get wet and cold, and my whole body would freeze. It was a great day when my mother bought me a pair of insulated boots.

Cold feet affect the whole body. There are churches in America that have frozen feet. They do not go with the gospel. Other interests have captured their attention. Some churches have cut back on giving to missions and other evangelism efforts to save money to build buildings. I am so glad I had the support of a godly deacon who agreed with me that while we were building our new church building we would continue to find ways to increase our missions giving. That young deacon would later mature into an elder and is now the pastor of Blessed Hope Bible Church, and he has led that church to even higher ground in the area of missions.

Most church growth in the American church is a result of church swapping or hopping. Eighty percent of new church members come from another church. The "go" in the gospel, for many people, means "go to church." Worse yet, it means go from church to church. We are not going with our feet with the gospel. The church is to be fishers of men. When fishermen do not fish they tend to fight. As a youngster my brother and I would go to my uncle's cabin on Bower's Beach in Delaware. We were there for the expressed purpose of going fishing on my uncle's boat. While we were out fishing, we would get along just fine. Once we were ashore and not fishing, we found ways to annoy each other and pick at each other. Eventually, we ended up fighting.

This is what so many of our churches do. We are too busy fishing for each other's faults instead of being fishers of men. We need to get our ugly feet thawed out and start running with the gospel.

I was working as the assistant pastor at Calvary Chapel in Staten Island with Pastor Lewis Nelms. I went there with my wife right out of college to help start the church. Lewis had already been there eight months before we joined him. My first priority upon my arrival was to knock on at least five hundred doors a week. Lewis had a map of Staten Island, and each week we would highlight every street we visited. Our goal was to reach out personally to every home on the island. Almost all the people in that church were won as new Christians. We met in an affluent part of the Staten Island, in the upstairs of a golf course country club every Sunday morning, Sunday evening, and Wednesday evening.

After eighteen months of winning and training these folks, Pastor Nelms made an announcement that we would no longer meet on Sunday night at the country club. We were instead going to the project area (poorer sections) on the north side of the island overlooking New York Harbor and the Statue of Liberty. Our church people had been reached with the good news and were being made into disciples. It was now their turn to run with the good news and teach others (2 Tim. 2:2).

We rented a Unitarian church that was well over a hundred years old. Lewis challenged us all not to just sit back but to go out into the highways and the hedges to compel the lost to come in. Lewis and I would knock on doors during the week to invite people to the service. Some of our church members would show up at that old church at 5 p.m. Sunday. We would kneel around the altar to pray and then go out to knock on doors to invite people to church. Hundreds came to Christ and are still serving Him. Church members would show up early for church, and I would give them an index card with a name and an address to pick up a person or family in the projects. They were not driving a church van or bus but a Cadillac, a BMW, a Mercedes, or whatever vehicle they drove. It was truly a miracle of compassion and love. These people had beautiful feet and a heart to share the love of Christ. The church was a mixture of young, old, rich, poor, black, white, Hispanic, Caribbean, and Asian. I was visiting that church recently, and it is a strong Bible-preaching church with a godly, dedicated pastor still reaching out to the lost. Praise the Lord that they finally have their own building. Many of the original families have since moved away, but most of them are still active church workers where God has transplanted them.

One teen girl and her mother were from Costa Rica. They become strong Christians. The teen girl would be our little daughter's first baby-sitter. Eventually she went off to Columbia Bible College for missions. She is now married and with children of her own. She and her husband have worked as a couple for InterVarsity most recently at Yale University, reaching and teaching the lost about Christ.

One of the people who was saved in that ministry and who helped pick up people for church and train them was a Jamaican mother. She went on to teach children and a ladies Bible study. She would host a Tuesday night prayer meeting at her house where six to ten of us would literally get on our faces and pray for hours. Blessed Hope Bible Church, the church I would later plant in Pennsylvania, was birthed from those prayer meetings. This dear woman's little girl would grow up and go off to Liberty University and on to Penn State and Dickinson Law School. She is now practicing law in Harrisburg, Pa., and is editing this book for me.

Another teenage boy, whose whole family was saved through Calvary Chapel and whose father was one of our first deacons, helped us reach out to his public high school with a club we started called Y.E.S.: Youth Excellent in Spirit. He also went off to Bible college. He has started a singles ministry on Staten Island called the Living Room, which is reaching people for Christ and encouraging many of the believers. He recently got married, and at his wedding several people gave testimony about his bold witness for Christ even as a teen in high school.

Thank God for a pastor who kept the feet of the church warm and moving toward reaching out to the lost. Perhaps our feet were not the most beautiful, but from what I have seen, they were at least pleasant in appearance.

### Why Should We Run with the Gospel?

*Sinners are perishing* (Ps. 9:17; Rev. 20:15; Mark 16:16; John 3:16). Knowing that people without Christ will go to hell should move us to action with compassion. Hell has not cooled off, no matter how many people ignore its existence. Everyone is on their way somewhere, whether it be heaven or hell.

*Love constrains us* (2 Cor. 5:14). Does it not concern us that billions are lost? Any person who has experienced the love of Christ in their heart will be moved with that love of others. Paul's love for his brethren, the Jews, was so great that he would be willing to be accursed if only he could reach his fellow kinsmen.

*God has commanded us* (Mark 16:15; Mark 5:19; Luke 14:23; Matt. 4:19; Acts 1:8). Not seeking the lost makes us guilty of disobeying a direct command from God.

*We have a God-given position that requires us* (2 Cor. 5:20; Luke 24:47). We are ambassadors for Christ. This is a sacred trust that we must carry out. We are obligated to speak on His behalf as citizens of that foreign country called heaven.

*Responsibility is pressing us* (Rom. 1:14; Ezek. 33:8; James 5:20). We are responsible for the lost around us. We are our brother's keeper. Paul said that we are a "debtor" to all types of people to give them the gospel of Christ.

*The fields of the world are calling us* (John 4:35; Matt. 9:37). Jesus tells us that the way to heaven is a narrow way and few will find it (Matt. 7:13-14). Then He tells (Matt. 9:37) that the harvest is plenteous and vast, but the laborers are few. So we have only a few laborers out of the few that have found salvation. It sounds as if we need every Christian to help with this job of world evangelism. Sixty million people will die this year, and over one hundred and thirty million will be born. That is a lot of people coming and going, and less than twenty percent of them have yet to know Christ in a saving way.

*The very nature of the gospel requires us* (Rom. 1:16). The word gospel means Good News! It is good news for sinners that Christ's death, burial, and resurrection can and will save them from penalty and power of sin. The nature of news is that it must be told. And Good News needs to be broadcasted and celebrated!

*Hell is requesting us* (Luke 16:27). The rich man who went to hell requested that someone go warn his family members not to end up there.

*Heaven is encouraging us* (Luke 15:5). The throne room of God rejoices when someone repents and trusts Christ. It is exciting to me to realize that we can add to the joy of the heavenly host as we share the gospel here.

*Joy is awaiting us* (Ps. 126:5-6; Luke 15:11-33). There is great joy in helping someone come to Christ and have their life changed. In the parable of the prodigal son, the whole household was able to join in the celebration of the son's return home. Charles H. Spurgeon said, "You only have one opportunity to enjoy the fatted calf of your own salvation, but you can join in the sharing of the fatted calf of others as you give out the Good News of the gospel."

*Time is challenging us* (Rom. 13:11-12; Eph. 5:15-17; James 4:13-17). Our lives are short, and we have only so much time to serve the Lord. We may not have tomorrow to get started, so we need to begin now. The life expectancies in some of the countries where Gospelink works are some of the lowest in the world. The life expectancy in the African nations of Malawi is thirty-six; Zambia, thirty-seven; and Zimbabwe; thirty-nine. Deadly diseases like AIDS and malaria are mocking us. Islam is actively and rapidly spreading its false doctrine. Time is challenging us!

*Paul demonstrated it for us* (Acts 20:20-21; Acts 20:26,31; 1 Cor. 2:2; 1 Cor. 3:6,9; 1 Cor. 9:22; Rom. 9:2-3). Paul was a man with a mission and never ceased to pursue it, even while he was in prison.

*The early church modeled it for us* (the book of Acts). The church grew numerically, geographically, and spiritually. They steadfastly met for prayer, fellowship, teaching of the Word, and the Lord's Supper. Every occasion was an opportunity to tell others about the gospel of Jesus Christ. Witnessing was a way of life and not just a church function or activity. Acts 2:1-47 shows us that great adding of people to the church came with a great anointing of the Holy Spirit.

*Jesus set the example for us* (Luke 19:10; Luke 4:18; Mark 2:14; John 4:4-26). The heartbeat of Jesus was winning people for the kingdom of God. His reason for birth, it was His substance for life and the purpose of His death. "Then said, Jesus to them again, Peace be unto you: as my Father hath sent me, even so send I you" (John 20:21). Jesus was sent by the Father in a certain way, and we are to be sent as He was. How was Jesus sent, and how are we to go?

## So Send I You

*Jesus was sent continually communicating with the Father in prayer*. Even His commissioning of the disciples was an answer to an earlier prayer (John 17:15-18). As we have already examined, Jesus was a person of prayer. We must go as prayer warriors.

*Jesus was sent as commissioned by the Father* (John 20:21). He did come and seek the lost out of love for us. However, if we look a bit closer and deeper we find His ultimate motivation was love for the Father and to bring glory to the Father (John 17:1). Mankind is not always lovable, but God the Father is. Hudson Taylor would tell prospective missionaries to China that a love for the Chinese people was not a sufficient reason to go there as a missionary. Only a deep, abiding love for God and His glory will sustain us. God is the only eternal constant in which to place our total faith, and He is the sender.

*Jesus was sent consecrated by the Spirit*. Jesus breathed on the disciples to represent their need for the power of the Spirit on their lives. Jesus did what He did in the power of the Spirit. This is most often manifested in the Gospel of Luke, which most frequently mentions the true humanity of Christ. We need unction to function for the Lord. I'll take this opportunity to repeat the need for personal and corporate holiness of the believers. He is called the Holy Spirit and does not rest His power on the unclean. The great Scottish preacher Robert Murray McCheyne said of his congregation, "One of my people's greatest needs is my own personal holiness."

The first book I ever received and read as a new Christian, apart from the Bible, was The Pursuit of Holiness by Jerry Bridges. Iris gave it to me when we first started dating. I remember reading it through the night on the train ride to Bible college. I highly recommend it to everyone interested in a study of holiness.

*Jesus was sent with compassion toward others* (Matt. 9:36-38). Jesus was not indifferent to the burdens of the people. He met many earthly needs for people. The more liberal churches for years only did the humanitarian aspect of the ministry, and many of us have criticized them for their lack of commitment to Bible truth. We are correct for pointing out this error, but the more fundamental churches have shown too little interest in the physical needs of people. I am grateful to the man who pastored my family for two of the years that I have been in mission work. The church is a growing congregation of almost sixteen hundred people. The membership has people from approximately forty different nationalities. The church is heavily involved in meeting all kinds of needs in that cross-culture community. There is a whole army of people who give up portions of their Saturdays and Sundays and help to feed the hungry, fix cars, and paint and fix up homes. It is a church deeply committed to foreign missions as well as local evangelism.

But the one thing that strikes me most is how generous that church has been with its buildings. There are at least four other churches that are allowed to use their facilities. It shows me an absence of pettiness and jealousy. There are not many pastors or churches who would be so kind and committed to God's kingdom. This pastor has a compassion for the souls of people and their burdens in this life. He has a tender heart and is willing to shed tears as Jesus did. His preaching has often stirred my heart and challenged me to higher ground.

Lord, lay some soul upon my heart,
And love that soul through me;
And may I always do my part,
To win that soul to Thee.

—Ira D. Sankey

The mission organization that I work with is Gospelink, and we are fervently committed to the salvation of souls in the poorest of countries by supporting hundreds of national pastors and their families. Our main objective has been, and still is, the proclamation of the gospel to the ends of the earth. But as we are doing that we are making an enormous difference in the quality of life for thousands of Christian brothers and sisters in economically challenged countries.

I am grateful for every America missionary who has given his or her life to serve on foreign fields. And in many places and cases they are still very necessary. However, we need to begin helping the native pastors of these poor countries. It is their homeland, their culture, and their language. And by helping them at their level of need we are able to help far more people in a compassionate way. Christ has commanded us to help the least of these. James 2:15-16 tells us that if a brother or sister is in need of the basic things in life and we ignore them, our faith is not real. What concerns me is how much mission money is going into the pockets of Americans, and so little of it is going overseas where it is so urgently needed. There is something terribly wrong, and it goes back to the churches and the need for honest compassion.

One day when I was having lunch with an American evangelist, we both had too much to eat. He was reaching for his third helping of food while complaining that a native pastor in Africa might take some of the money he received and buy extra rice to share with his brother and his family. I was grieved that this should be such a concern to him, and I told him as much. We have well over fifty percent of the world's wealth in America, with less than five percent of the world's population. Sometimes I am ashamed of how little I do to help others who have so little, and I am frustrated with our sanctimonious excuses for our greed. God help us to be more compassionate.

*Jesus was sent at a great cost to self* (John 20:20). Before our Lord commissioned the disciples in verse 21, He identified Himself by the scars on His body in verse 20. How was Jesus sent by the Father? At a great cost and sacrifice. What does it cost us to serve Christ? What do we sacrifice for the sake of the gospel? In 1991, I was speaking to a foreign missionary from Eastern Europe. He told me that the Muslim world will never be reached without a great number of western martyrs willing to lay down their lives for the sake of the gospel. I must admit, even though I greatly admire this man, I believed he was exaggerating. Since the events of September 11, 2001, I no longer disagree with him; instead, I see his words as rather prophetic in nature.

In America, we take our religious freedom for granted. The rest of the church in the rest of the world has suffered far more than we have for their faith. Is the American church prepared to make the sacrifices to reach the Muslim world? How many of our churches are sending out missionaries? I do know some that are, and they are making incredible investments in the kingdom of God by their wise stewardship. They are more fully committed to making their missionaries a genuine extension of their church. Unfortunately, most of the churches in America give less then ten percent to missions. And only a percentage of that goes overseas. The Lord will not hold us guiltless for this selfish inequity. The mindset that has generated this self-indulgence originates with the man-centered mentality that says, "The church exists to meet my needs." This flies in the face of how Jesus was sent: "For ye know the grace of our Lord Jesus Christ, that, though He was rich, yet for our sakes He became poor, that ye through His poverty might be rich" (2 Cor. 8:9).

*Jesus was sent with great conviction and commitment to the Word of God.* Jesus stood on the principles of God's Word. Even here in John 20:23 Jesus called sin, sin and noted that it needed to be forgiven not trivialized. We read time and again Jesus saying, "It is written..." Jesus had compassionate love, but not at the expense His loyalty to the truth of the Bible.

*Jesus was sent to a community to serve.* We often quote the fact that Jesus came to save the world, and this is very true. But when Jesus came into the world He came and lived in a very small segment of that world. Jesus was born in Bethlehem Ephratah, a small town. He was reared in Nazareth, not a very distinguished city. Jesus came and served within a particular community of people. God has placed all of us in a particular place of service. No matter where you are planted by God, you are to grow and serve the Lord and others right there. Your feet are to carry you to your neighborhood, to your friends, and to your family. I have stated previously that churches need to see more missionaries go out from their ranks, but most people are called to serve as a missionary right in their hometown.

Jesus came to the shore of Gadarene where he met a man who was possessed by a legion of demons. This man was naked, living among the tombs, crying, and cutting himself. No one wanted to go near him, but our Lord approached him and cast the demons out of him. The man was now in his right mind, clothed, and volunteering to go to the mission field. He wanted to climb in the boat and go with Jesus, but what did Jesus tell him? "Go home to thy friends, tell them how great things the Lord hath done for thee, and hath compassion on thee" (Mark 5:19). Jesus told him to let his feet take him back to his family and friends. And you know what he did? "And he departed, and published in Decapolis how great things Jesus had done for him: and all men did marveled" (Mark 5:20).

*Jesus was sent to a community to serve.* The man from Gadarene was sent to his community to serve and spread the good news. The feet of most Christians will never carry them to foreign soil as a missionary. Neither should they. Most of us are called to the community where we live every day. It is required of us to simply go to the sphere of people where God has sent us. The Lord of the harvest is Jesus Christ. The children of the kingdom are the good seed, and the world is the field. The Lord plants His children where He wants them (Matt. 13:37-38). Go to your field and grow in your field.

No foreign missionary is any more special than several of the godly widowed women I know who have hardly ever left Perry County, Pennsylvania. They pray for missions. They pray for missionaries. They support missionaries with their very meager means. One supports two national pastors in Africa. They pray for their families, their churches, and their lost neighbors. Their feet are old and not as sturdy as they used to be, but to God, their feet are beautiful.

The Vaccaro family was one of the first families that came to church at Calvary Chapel in Staten Island. Gene, Barbara, and their children professed Christ, were baptized, and joined the church. They are the epitome of character, hard work, and service. They are soft-spoken, gentle and meek. They were witnesses for the Lord and students of the Scriptures, and their children were a joy to be around. Gene was our first deacon. Barbara was one of our first Sunday school teachers and nursery workers. Being a deacon at Calvary Chapel was not a position for the faint of heart. Because we had no building of our own, we had to set up all of our chairs and equipment for every service. Gene and Barbara were usually the first people there and often the last to leave.

A couple of years ago Barbara went into the hospital for a rather routine operation. The doctor made a horrible mistake and left Barbara paralyzed. She is bound to a wheelchair, with no use of her legs and very little use of her hands. Barb has volunteered to help us at Gospelink by reading the letters that come in. She is doing what she can to still serve the kingdom of God. Gene had to take an early retirement, and they sold their New York home and moved to rural

Pennsylvania. Gene's community of service has been drastically narrowed to his home, serving his dear wife. He must plan every detail of their lives by taking into consideration things we often take for granted. As Barbara's feet will no longer carry her, Gene's feet must serve her. That is where God has Gene serving, and he has been faithful. He is one of my heroes. I believe God looks at Gene's feet and says "How beautiful."

# So Send I You

So send I you, to labor unrewarded,
To serve unpaid, unloved, unsought, unknown,
To bear rebuke, to suffer scorn and scoffing—
So send I you, to toil for Me alone.

So send I you, to bind the bruised and broken,
O'er wandering souls to work, to weep, to wake,
To bear the burdens of a world a-weary—
So send I you, to suffer for My sake.

So send I you, to loneliness and longing,
With heart a hungering for the loved and unknown,
Forsaking home and kindred, friend and dear one—
So send I you, to know My love alone.

So send I you, to leave your life's ambition,
To die to dear desire, self-will resign,
To labor long, and love where men revile you—
So send I you to lose your life in Mine.

So send I you, to hearts made hard by hatred,
To eyes made blind because the will not see,
To spend, tho' it be blood, to spend and spare not—
So send I you, to taste of Calvary.

—E. Margaret Clarkson

# Can These Dry Bones Live?

The hand of the LORD was upon me, and carried me out in the spirit of the LORD, and set me down in the midst of the valley which was full of bones, And caused me to pass by them round about: and, behold, there were very many in the open valley; and, lo, they were very dry.

And he said unto me, Son of man, can these bones live? And I answered, O Lord GOD, thou knowest. Again he said unto me, Prophesy upon these bones, and say unto them, O ye dry bones, hear the word of the LORD. Thus saith the Lord GOD unto these bones; Behold, I will cause breath to enter into you, and ye shall live.—Ezek. 37:1-5

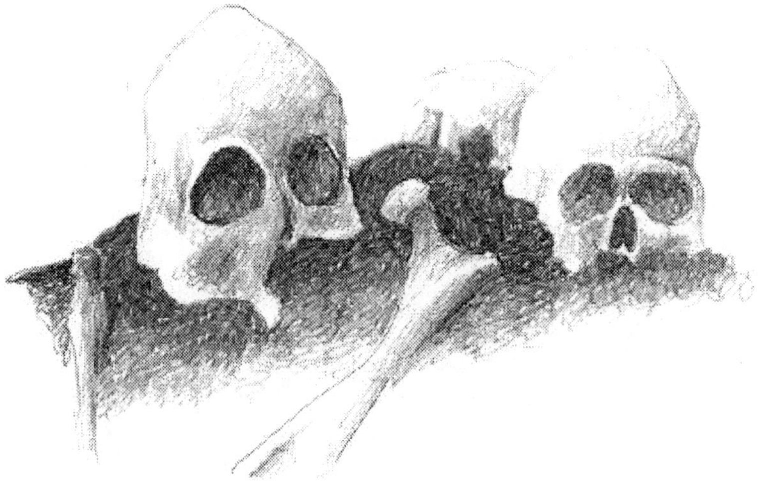

# Conclusion

# Can These Dry Bones Live?

A baby's body has three hundred "soft" bones at birth. These eventually fuse to form the two hundred six bones that adults have. Some of a baby's bones are made of a special material called cartilage. This cartilage is soft and flexible. During childhood, as you are growing, the cartilage grows and is slowly replaced by bone, with help from calcium.

By the time you are twenty-five, this process will be complete. After this, there can be no more growth—the bones are as big as they will ever be. All of these bones make up a skeleton that is both very strong and very light. These bones form a sturdy frame for the rest of our body and also help to protect our vital organs.

If you've ever seen a real skeleton or fossil in a museum, you might think that all bones are dead. Although bones in museums are dry, hard, or crumbly, the bones in your body are different. The bones that make up your skeleton are all very much alive, changing all the time like other parts of your body. In the very core of your bones is the jelly-like material called marrow. This actually produces your blood cells.

When a person's dead body decomposes, the last part of the body to disintegrate is the bones. The body may be long dead, but the bones can last many years beyond the actual death. So too, the dead or dying church can be full of spiritually dead people who are simply dried-up spiritual skeletons. This brings us to the setting in

Ezekiel 37, over twenty-five hundred years ago, in which the prophet Ezekiel is given a vision of a valley of dry bones.

Ezekiel was living in Babylon as a captive in exile. The city of Jerusalem had fallen, and the whole nation of Israel had been destroyed and scattered. The Israelites in Babylon felt their nation was dead. God's prophecy through Ezekiel was to "the whole house of Israel," which was being held captive. Israel had "died," and there was no hope. The vision of the dry bones is a prophecy of the restoration of Israel to her land when the greater son of David will reign as king and all Israel will "have one shepherd." The reviving of these dead bones signified Israel's national restoration. It depended on God's power alone for a national and a spiritual restoration. The breath of new life in the dead corpses symbolized the work of the Holy Spirit (Ezek. 36:24-28).The interpretation of this passage is the miracle-working of God to restore the dead nation of Israel to its homeland and spiritual roots, but there is a far broader application for us. This same powerful God is our God, and He can revive and restore our church and individual lives. In Ezekiel 37:3, the Lord asked, "Can these bones live?" Ezekiel wisely replies, "O Lord God, Thou knowest" (Ezek. 37:3).

By calling and sending a prophet to the dry bones, God in His sovereign grace initiates Israel's revival. The Lord sends His preacher to His people. This is often how the Lord begins revival. An evangelist, a pastor, teacher, or spiritual leader challenges God's people. Perhaps there is such a person reading this book, and God is calling you to call your church to revival. Obey His command. You must not be an ear-tickler or a man-pleaser; you must only fear God. Have a passion for God and a compassion for people.

The second scene, in which the bones become bodies, features the Word of God, thereby giving us our second insight into revival. It is the Word of the Lord that changes people. As you have read this book I pray that you have read the Scriptures quoted, and have looked up and read the hundreds verses that have been cited. If we are to have revival in our churches it must be based on the truth of the Bible. We must be transformed by the renewing of our minds to understand God's perfect will as revealed in His perfect Word.

The third scene, the wind reviving the slain bodies, features the role of God's Spirit, providing our third insight into revival. The Holy Spirit must breathe upon the people of the church. The lost must be regenerated or born from above (John 3:3; Eph. 2:1-6). God's people are made refreshed and revived by the Holy Spirit. The people of God are filled with the Spirit so as to be overwhelmingly aware of God's presence. They are eager to worship Him and to tell others about Him.

Can a dead church be revived? Yes, it can. Will it be revived? Only God knows! Revival is a sovereign act of God. However, human responsibility calls us to reformation. Reform sets things right that are wrong. It lays aside those things that are sinful. It begins to do those things that are right and commanded by God.

An Old Testament example of revival is King Josiah of Judah. He became king at the age of eight when his country was very far from God and was dead spiritually. At the age of sixteen he began his reform of the nation of Judah. He tore down all the idols and the altars where they were worshiped. He restored the house of God and reestablished the Passover celebration. He eventually located a copy of the Book of the Law, a scroll containing the Torah, God's revelation through Moses. Josiah commanded that the Word of God be read and obeyed. There was a great yearning for God's honor and glory (2 Kings 22-23; 2 Chronicles 34–35).

Josiah teaches us that we must be faithful to carry out our human responsibilities before the Lord. Many of us talk about revival and wanting to see God revive our churches, but what do we mean by revival? Do we think of revival as our churches full of people singing, laughing, working, giving, building, going? Many people want God to give them and their church what they believe are the fruits of revival without deliberately seeking to reform their behavior to what they know God's Word says.

Reformation and revival are companions. We must seek to set things right that we know are wrong. This is reformation. I trust that is what the previous chapters in this book have encouraged you to do. Get back to the basics of reading, studying, and meditating on the Word of God. Be faithful to pray privately, corporately, and effectively on a regular basis. Trust the Lord more fully and be careful not to let your heart get hardened. Be aware of the enemy, Satan, and put on the whole armor of God. Keep the soil of your heart prepared to hear from God and beware of having itching ears for the vain philosophies of men. We must keep our compassion for those around us and our vision on God's kingdom work. May God the Holy Spirit control our tongue and may our feet be beautifully swift to run to our community and beyond with the gospel.

Most of us know far more Bible than we obey. We often need reminders to be faithful to the commands that are already very familiar to us. Many years ago I heard a preacher make a comment that I have often recalled. He was giving his opinion about why a particular well-known pastor was so successful in reaching and teaching people. He wisely observed that one reason for this man's success was his willingness to proclaim and repeat the obvious. There is certainly nothing wrong with the deep and the profound, but they should never come at the expense or exclusion of the basics.

Every effort should be made to reform our lives and our churches according to the basics. What about revival? As God the Holy Spirit moves in a special way, we will see a hunger for God. The psalmist reflects on the ultimate goal and fruit of God-given revival when he states, "Wilt thou not revive us again: that Thy people may rejoice in Thee?" (Ps. 85:6). Do you see it? When God revives us He is the focal point. He does not just give us joy, but He is our joy! Worship, the worthiness of God, becomes our daily obsession and not just a weekly ritual.

King Solomon's final words of advice, in Ecclesiastes 12:9-14, provide a fitting conclusion. Even in Solomon's time there were scores of books being written, with Solomon having not only read many but also authored some. This is how he summed up his writings:

> And moreover, because the preacher [Solomon] was wise, he still taught the people knowledge; yea, he gave good heed, and sought out, and set in order many proverbs. The preacher sought to find out acceptable words: and that which was written was upright, even words of truth.

> The words of the wise are as goads [prods], and as nails fastened by the masters of assemblies [truth firmly fixes itself in our mind], which are given from one Shepherd [God is the source of true wisdom]. And further, by these, my son, be admonished [be careful not to add more to the Shepherd's truth]: of making many books there is no end; and much study is a weariness of the flesh.
>
> Let us hear the conclusion of the whole matter: Fear God, and keep his commandments: for this is the whole duty of man. For God shall bring every work into judgment, with every secret thing, whether it be good, or whether it be evil.

I first read these words on the very night I trusted Jesus Christ as my Savior on March 22, 1980, and they have helped to anchor my soul for these many years. There is a God, and He knows everything we think, say, and do. He alone shall judge us. To God alone be the glory forever and ever. Amen!

# Revive Us Again

We praise Thee, O God! For the Son of Thy love,
For Jesus who died, and is now gone above.

We praise Thee, O God! For Thy Spirit of light,
Who has shown us our Savior, and scattered our night.

All glory and praise to the Lamb, that was slain,
Who has borne all our sins, and hath cleansed every stain.

Revive us again; fill each heart with Thy love;
May each soul be rekindled with fire from above.

Hallelujah! Thine the glory, Hallelujah! Amen;
Hallelujah! Thine the glory, revive us again.

—William P. MacKay

# Resources: Preventive Prescriptions

**Proverbs 11:14** "Where no counsel is, the people fall: but in the multitude of counselors there is safety."

Holy Bible by God

*A Call to Spiritual Reformation: Prayers of Paul* by D.A. Carson
*Ashamed of the Gospel* by John F. MacArthur
*Basic Theology* by Charles C. Ryrie
*Christian Theology* by Millard J. Erickson
*Counterfeit Revival* by Hank Hanegraaff
*Escape From Reason* by Francis A. Schaeffer
*Evangelism Explosion* by Dr. D.J. Kennedy
*Fresh Wind, Fresh Fire* by Jim Cymbala
*Gospelink- Helping National Preachers* by Lewis Nelms @ www.gospelink.org
*He Is There and He Is Not Silen*t by Francis A. Schaeffer
*Holiness* by Henry Blackaby
*Holiness* by J.C. Ryle
*Knowing God* by J.I. Packer
*Leading a World Missions Church* by Dr. Jerry Kroll @ Heritage Baptist Church (434) 237-6505
*Let the Nations be Glad: Supremacy of God in Missions* by John Piper
*Mere Christianity* by C.S. Lewis
*Mind Renewal in a Mindless Age* by James M. Boice

*No Place for Truth, Or Whatever Happen to Evangelical Theology* by David F. Wells
*Orthodoxy and Heresy: Where to Draw the Line* by Joel E. Parkinson
*Our Accountability To God: The Nature of Fallen Man* by A.W. Pink
*Our Sufficiency in Chris*t by John F. MacArthur
*Revival* by Martyn Lloyd-Jones
*Revival and Revivalism: The Making and Marring of American Evangelism* by Iain Murray
*Revive Us Again: Biblical Insights for Renewal* by Walter C. Kaiser
*Sermons on Sovereignty* by Charles H. Spurgeon
*Sharpening the Focus of the Church* by Gene A. Getz
*Spiritual Leadership* by J. Oswald Sanders
*Standing on the Rock - Biblical Authority* by James M. Boice
*Teaching On Preaching* by Jack Hyles
*The Battle for the Beginning: Creation, Evolution, and the Bible* by John F. MacArthur
*The Bible Expositional Commentary Old Testament & New Testament* by Warren W. Wiersbe
*The Celebration Hymnal: Songs and Hymns for Worship* by Word Music / Integrity Music
*The God Who Is There* by Francis A. Schaeffer
*The Nature of God* by A.W. Pink
*The Pleasures of God in Being God* by John Piper
*The Purpose Driven Church* by Rick Warren
*The Purpose Driven Life* by Rick Warren
*The Pursuit of God* by A.W. Tozer
*The Pursuit of Holiness* by Jerry Bridges
*The Pursuit of Man: The Divine Conquest of the Human Heart* by A.W. Tozer
*The Sovereignty of God* by A.W. Pink
*The Supremacy of God in Preaching* by John Piper
*Visioneering: God's Blueprint for Developing and Maintaining Personal Vision* by Andy Stanley
*When People Are Big and God Is Small* by Edward T. Welch
*Why Good People Do Bad Things* by Erwin W. Lutzer

*Why the Cross Can Do What Politics Can't* by Erwin W. Lutzer
*Your Mind Matters* by John R.W. Stott

* It should be noted that the author does not endorse everything written in all these books. The reader is to use their God given discernment. That said, there is much spiritual gold to be gleaned out of these books

Lou Mancari is available to do pulpit supply with a wide range of topics. He primarily addresses local churches on the subject of foreign missions, revival, and family life issues. (434)384-1232 or (434)384-2008 or email lmancari@gospelink.org or loumancari@yahoo.com.

Pastors and teachers may purchase a CD with a power point outline that covers the material in this book. Many graphics and Bible references are ready to assist you in teaching all or any part of this book. 45 slides that can be edited as suits the user.

Send $10.00 to Lou Mancari
3013 Cardinal Place
Lynchburg, VA 24503

Or call one of the phone numbers above.
Please include your name and address with your order.

Printed in the United States
63116LVS00003B/186